In Our Dreams We Read

Stories from the front lines of literacy

By Bruce K. Berger

Foreword by Margaret Doughty,
Founder, Literacy Powerline

Photography by Nickerson B. Miles

Published by WordWorthyPress, LLC
Northport, Alabama

Photographs and book design by Nickerson B. Miles

The body type is set in Constantia, headers and
highlights in Tahoma

Cover design by Michael Wilson,
MichaelWilsonDesign, Charlotte, NC
mwdstudio@bellsouth.net

ISBN 978-0-9855048-0-9

Library of Congress Control Number: 2012944226
Library of Congress subject headings:
    Adult illiteracy
    Costs of illiteracy
    Front lines of literacy
    Functional illiteracy
    Illiteracy
    Literacy
    Literacy and community engagement
    Literacy and self achievement
    Literacy service providers
    Personal stories of literacy
    Reading tutor

Table of contents

This book is dedicated to
40 million American adults
who dream of reading,
and to the tutors and teachers
who patiently breathe life
into those dreams.

Foreword

IN my work as a literacy coalition builder I have never seen such an uplifting collection of stories celebrating those who want to learn and those who volunteer to teach them to read. These unique stories shine a spotlight on the people who make a difference all over this country, those who build up the confidence of those failed or forgotten by the system and those determined to build a new life for themselves and their families by improving their reading and writing.

I met Dr. Bruce Berger for the first time at a community summit when the West Alabama area was beginning to shine a spotlight on the impact of low literacy in the counties surrounding Tuscaloosa. There was a spirit of energy and passion in the summit—people wanted to help, wanted to make a difference. The second time I met Bruce was in a board meeting of the Literacy Council of West Alabama. The board was talking about statistics, shocked by the facts and appalled by the poverty, unable to get their arms around the intergenerational implications of how low literacy promotes poverty, poor health and under-employment. Bruce started talking about action—about what his students were doing and how they were focused on making a difference. His approach was positive, uplifting and grounded in community organizing.

There are serious community issues we face in this country, but very few are easily changed. This series of stories explores simple solutions to the foundational problem of low literacy. Literacy is the one tool that can take an individual from challenge to success and a community to economic prosperity. These stories show how we can all be part of the solutions and we can all give the gift of learning.

Alabama is not the only state challenged in this way, but it is a state with a history that has compounded low literacy, a state with huge rural tracts with poor transportation and communication systems and limited resources.

On April 27, 2011, I was stepping onto a plane from Houston on my way to Tuscaloosa, just about to turn off my phone when it rang and literacy coalition director Stephen Bridgers asked if I could still get off the plane; he said bad weather was on the way, and our meetings were canceled. I waited till the evening to hear the news: The worst tornadoes in living record hit, and the region was devastated.

President Obama declared Alabama a major disaster area, clearing the way for federal aid to help families who lost homes or businesses and local governments that sustained damage to public property. All nine counties in the literacy coalition region were in the federal disaster zone. Families were displaced, schools destroyed, houses flattened and services severely devastated.

Those with the lowest skills were impacted by an inability to read and comprehend the FEMA paperwork, challenged to fully take advantage of emergency health care, unable to read informed consent documents and understand treatment options. Many, especially the unbanked, faced a financial literacy challenge after receiving federal aid and not quite understanding how to spend the funds. The tornado dramatically served to spotlight the issue of low literacy even more forcefully.

Volunteers were organized through the network of nonprofit, civic and faith-based organizations to assist those with limited literacy skills to complete FEMA applications, enroll children in summer schools and fill out insurance paperwork. These same providers had lost offices, materials, resources and were themselves severely challenged to provide their services.

Bruce says he is troubled deeply by low literacy—so are the thousands across the country who work with those with limited literacy skills. Yet, why is there no march for literacy or public uprising or national campaign? That is why this book is so very important to share the experiences of learners and tutors who are making such a difference and changing lives for the better across the country. Thank you, Bruce, for helping to make the world a better place by improving literacy levels and giving the gift of learning.

— Margaret Doughty
Member of the British Empire and
Founder, Literacy Powerline
January 2012

"We do not need another study [of literacy].
We do not need a new commission.
We know exactly what needs to be done.
We do not have the right to find retreat in
earnest indecision.
We have the obligation to take action."

— Jonathan Kozol
   Illiterate America, p. 101

Prologue:
What would your life be like if you couldn't read?

If you live in Alabama, the inability to read means this: a 30 percent chance you dropped out of school, a 40 percent chance you live in poverty, a 50 percent chance you are unemployed and a good chance that you have stacked time in jail or prison, abused drugs or alcohol or otherwise lived life on the edge.

I only learned later in life that literacy isn't a gift given to all. Reading was never optional in my childhood. My mother was a schoolteacher and a fierce advocate for reading. My father was an electrician who devoured newspapers and western novels and addicted me to crossword puzzles at a young age. I still recall collections of books and magazines scattered throughout the house and, in the living room, a blonde bookcase that sagged under the weight of an *Encyclopedia Britannica* and scores of back issues of the *Reader's Digest*. My sister, brother and I gathered for nightly bedtime stories and trekked each week to the township library to reload with new stories.

My first job at age eight was a morning newspaper route. The papers I delivered—the *Detroit Free Press* and Chicago's *Sun Times* and *Tribune*—illuminated people and events far beyond the horizon of our small village in southern Michigan. They fed my imagination and fueled my dreams. The heavy bundle of newspapers arrived each morning at 4:30, signaled by a perpetually squealing belt on the panel delivery truck.

Bruce K. Berger

In the kitchen I'd fold the thick papers and tuck them into the delivery bag while my mother offered opinions on the headlines and events of the world. She never lacked for opinions, or warm hugs to send me on my route.

For an hour I'd bicycle through town pitching newspapers on porches, inciting neighborhood dogs to frenzy, and racing against the first light of a new day. It was a grand job, and I loved the smell and heft of newspapers then, their promising weight and the wonder of columnar words that magically came to life in reading. I still do.

I first encountered illiteracy at sprawling army bases in Kentucky and Louisiana in the late 1960s, and then it smacked me in the face in Vietnam. One of my buddies—we called him Sunshine because of his engaging, ever-present smile—couldn't read. So when mail arrived, Sunshine designated me as his reader. Four or five times I read each letter aloud while he discussed and memorized its contents.

Sunshine was from Louisiana, 18, married and the father of a baby girl. Another baby was on the way, and most of his letters were from his wife, Jumelle, who wrote him each week. Her letters were warm, religious, deeply personal. I admired her faith and strength. Occasionally, Sunshine asked me to help him write a letter to Jumelle. He said he couldn't read because he and his teachers just never got around to it. Besides, his mother couldn't read, and he'd never met his father. He told us that Jumelle would teach him to read when he returned to the real world. I hope that happened. I lost track of Sunshine when he was wounded and evacuated to a hospital out of country.

Several years later I met Bob in a conversational German class at a community college in southern Michigan. I'd taken a position there as an English instructor following my tour of Vietnam and a year of graduate studies. Many of my students, like Bob, were adults with children and families of their own. They viewed education as an opportunity for a better job in a difficult economy in the mid 1970s. They all wanted to get ahead of wherever they were. Bob was in his 50s, a truck driver, married and the father of three. That first night in class I asked the students to complete an information form, which included several open-ended questions about their interest in learning German. Bob rose and approached me as the other students completed the forms.

"I don't understand these questions," he said.

"Let's look at the first one," I suggested. "Tell me what you don't understand?"

"The whole damn thing," he said. "I can't read it. I never learned to read much. I can only read in my dreams."

This book is a collection of brief stories about adults like Bob and Sunshine who dream of reading, and the tutors, teachers and service providers or connectors who help them realize their dreams. According to ProLiteracy, the largest organization of adult reading programs in the world, more than 40 million American adults can't read, or they are functionally illiterate, which means they lack basic reading, writing and math skills necessary in everyday life. They can't complete a job application, understand warnings on prescription drug labels, write checks to pay bills, or even apply for a hunting or fishing license. They survive in a world of print that is as undecipherable as a foreign language.

Illiteracy troubles me deeply. How can it be that 40 million adults in the U.S. can't read, or that 20 percent of our high school seniors are functionally illiterate when they formally cross the stage to graduate (Educa-tion-Portal.com, July 27, 2007)? As a country that prides itself on education for all, how has this hap-pened? What's life like for the millions of adults who can't read, and what are the implications for those in the future who are unable to read? How will they deal with a rapidly changing world that is hurtling into an unknown future? What does it mean for democracy and an informed citizenry? What can we do about it?

Twenty-five years ago Jonathan Kozol (1985) raised the alarm on illiteracy in his haunting book, *Illiterate America*. He argued compellingly that functional illit-eracy touches all Americans because it is deeply linked with crime, unemployment, poverty, high school drop-out rates, low voting rates and other social, economic and political ills that afflict our communities and workplaces, diminish our collective national literacy and threaten the nation's future. But few paid atten-tion, apparently, because the number of adults (and children) who can't read continues to increase while our collective national literacy continues to sink. Today the U.S. ranks 51st in literacy among member countries in the United Nations (Cleckler, 2008) We are not a literacy superpower.

One problem is that functional illiteracy is often invisible. It certainly isn't a sexy issue. It doesn't wear suggestive clothing, smile seductively or catch your eye with bling. You won't see it featured in prime time television programs or popular YouTube videos. And it's generally not the stuff of novels, songs or movies, though Quinton Aaron and Sandra Bullock gave it a Hollywood face in the film, *The Blind Side*.

We also don't see illiteracy because we don't know or understand its signs, though they are easy to learn. For example, someone struggles to understand the contents of a canned or boxed food in a supermarket, or asks for help finding a particular food. Or an individual asks you or the clerk in a shop or store for help in writing a check because he forgot his glasses. These are a few of the signs.

Those who can't read also have developed powerful coping skills. They educate themselves through their own experiences and the stories and oral histories of others. They gather news and information from listening to the radio, watching television or talking with others. Sometimes they pretend they can read. They don't want to tell others they can't read because they often find this embarrassing, and they are proud individuals. They work, raise families and belong to groups and organizations. They possess values, beliefs and hopes for a brighter future. They've made it through life so far without being able to read, and they'll just keep on keeping on.

But illiteracy often carries heavy personal, social and economic costs. A disproportionate number of those who can't read live in the margins of society where poverty and hunger are companions, jobs are more difficult to find, crime is prevalent and drug and alcohol abuse are all too common. Many studies have shown that illiteracy is deeply linked to these and other stubborn social and economic issues. The problem is serious in Alabama, where the Literacy Council of West Alabama and the State Literacy Workforce and Development Council report that:

- 600,000 to 1,000,000 Alabama residents, or 16-25 percent of the population, are functionally illiterate. The rates are higher in some West Alabama counties.
- 40 percent of Alabama's fourth graders are unable to read at grade level, and 40 percent of fourth graders don't graduate from high school.
- 55 percent of Alabama's adults function at literacy levels unable to meet the demands of a modern technical society.
- 70 percent of Alabama's prison inmates are functionally illiterate.
- 75 percent of small business owners in Alabama report that many applicants for job openings lack basic reading, writing and math skills. They are unable to complete job applications.

So I wrote this book, and Nick Miles took these photographs, to put some real faces on Alabama's literacy struggles. We wanted to personalize illiteracy because we believe people are more likely to understand a problem and engage it when they can see the faces and hear the voices of people closest to the problem. Walt Fisher (1978, 1987) challenged the idea that people are mostly rational creatures who make decisions and take actions based on logical and factual evidence. He argued that people also are valuing in nature: They can be moved to action and powerfully influenced by stories and personal dramas. Stories are at the root of human experience. They help us form communities of identification and create rituals that may lead to shared views and collective actions. We learn through stories, and we bond and build relationships through them. Stories can seize our hearts.

In 2010-11, then, I interviewed and gathered the stories of 30 people in four communities in central and west Alabama—Bessemer, Birmingham, Hoover and Tuscaloosa. This diverse group of men and women, ranging in age from 13-72, shared their personal stories and spoke candidly about how reading intersects their lives as students and learners, tutors or service providers. Their personal accounts depict struggles, failures, successes and most of all hope—hope for a better life and a brighter future for themselves and others. That's why I choose to have them speak for themselves. The stories capture their respective voices and speaking styles, replete with grammatical errors.

I am deeply indebted to these 30 people for opening their hearts and sharing their experiences and dreams.

These brief stories are organized around six themes that resonate in their accounts: redemption, commitment, obligation, opportunity, discovery and community. Stories of *redemption* are shared by those who have lived on the edge and who now reach for literacy to gain a second chance. Kimberly in Birmingham, HIV positive herself, wants to improve her reading so that she can better help AIDS patients complete paperwork for their counseling sessions at a local center where she works part time. Robert, a young adult in Bessemer who has wrestled with his own drug addiction demons for more than half of his 26 years, believes the act of tutoring is as important to him as it is to his teenage student. Neil, a retiree, teaches a class in accelerated learning at a maximum-security prison near Bessemer and believes that reading not only improves lives, but saves them.

A deep *commitment* to fighting illiteracy characterizes the stories of others who have served on the front lines for many years. Dick Sweeney teaches in a multicultural resource center in Hoover; he believes the ability to read is a form of freedom. Miss Tommie, a long-time tutor in Birmingham, contends that we have to learn to read the signs of those who can't read, and then we have to enter their lives to help them. Julia at Shelton State Community College in Tuscaloosa has worked in adult education for many years because the need is so acute. She still thrills at witnessing adults who learn to read, day by day.

Others feel an *obligation* to pass on the gift of literacy to others. Charnessa and LaTonya in Bessemer want to be able to read to their young children and help them eventually with their homework. Reading provides their children with an opportunity they did not have. Steve, who works at the Literacy Council in Birmingham, was a tennis professional who came to believe that illiteracy is everyone's problem. He quit the tennis court to fight illiteracy full time. Tiffany, an adult tutor, thinks obligations run the other way, too: Those who need reading help should take advantage of the opportunities they have to learn to read.

Six of the stories highlight *opportunity* as a central theme—the chance to get ahead. Steven in Tuscaloosa wants to improve his reading skills so that he can enter a GED program, learn a mechanical trade and someday own an auto body shop. David, who now delivers appliances for a living, also wants to own a business—a lawnmower repair shop. He believes he is a genius on lawnmowers. Yolanda loves to travel and hopes to become a long-distance trucker. Tavarus sees the world as a series of tests one must successfully complete to get ahead, and you can't pass the tests if you can't read.

Stories of *discovery* reveal how individuals have come to engage the issue of literacy. Cheryl in Birmingham claims that the encouragement of her tutor, and the love she feels in the company of those in her church provide the courage she needs to continue to develop her reading ability. Mary Lena in Tuscaloosa became a tutor after personally witnessing how difficult life is for those who can't read, and how they are sometimes the recipients of discrimination. Dave, 70, was a career Air Force pilot and a high school math teacher in Atlanta before he "retired" and subsequently launched an adult reading program at the Public Library in Bessemer in 2009. He was moved to do this because he discovered the need was so overwhelming.

Literacy is also linked to voting patterns, civic participation and quality of life in neighborhoods and communities. Four stories of *community* emphasize this theme. José, a musician who relocated from California to Alabama, wants to read and speak English so he can become a "real part" of the American culture, of which he and his family are very proud. Jackie, former chair of the Literacy Council of West Alabama, believes that literacy can only be eradicated if every group and organization embraces the issue and incorporates it in its goals and programs. Johnnie, previously president of the Chamber of Commerce of West Alabama, argues that the economic future of the country is tied deeply to the literacy of its people. He calls for the business community in West Alabama to get behind the issue because the U.S. has lost its competitive edge in the global marketplace and is falling behind many other countries in terms of literacy rates.

These stories represent just a few of the thousands of individuals who serve on the front lines of literacy in Alabama. The front lines are the libraries, classrooms, churches, community service centers, literacy houses and day-care centers where people connect to one another around the idea that the ability to read and understand words is crucial to an enriched life for individuals, families, workplaces, communities and nations. In addition, hundreds of service provider organizations across the state offer support and assistance with basic reading development, General Education Degree (GED) preparation, English as a Second Language (ESL) programs and education programs for adults and low-income and at-risk students, among others. Service providers or connectors are a diverse group, including groups and organizations like M-POWER Ministries in Birmingham, the largest adult literacy program in the state; Bevill State, Shelton State and other community colleges in Alabama; the Multicultural Resources Center in Hoover; and numerous community and county development programs across the state.

Fundamentally, these programs are designed to help individuals improve reading and writing skills and advance their education. Literacy is not the goal of such programs, but rather it is the skill that is developed to provide a foundation for self-achievement. Literacy skills are the tools that allow people to enrich their lives and improve employment opportunities. Literacy empowers people to participate more fully in their own governance, and to pare down and reduce poverty, crime, hunger, the spread of diseases and human rights abuses, among other social problems.

The inability to read, of course, is not unique to residents of Alabama, and the stories in this book are but a handful of millions of such stories across the country. Illiteracy has no address. It doesn't discriminate by age, race, gender, religion or geography. It lives in teeming inner cities, sprawling suburbs, rural villages and farmlands, and in mountains, forests and deserts around the world. It is truly a global problem, and ProLiteracy estimates that nearly 800 million adults worldwide are illiterate in their native languages, and nearly two billion people can't read.

As people in the Alabama stories suggest, the costs of illiteracy are extraordinarily high. The inability to read, write, do basic math, manage essential financial transactions and understand technologies impacts the quality of individual lives and stunts human potential. It affects relationships, families and workplaces. It reduces the prosperity and health of communities. It limits the extent to which citizens can engage in their communities and participate in the governance of their lives. It diminishes the rich possibilities of democracy.

In the end, the literacy problem is everybody's problem, not somebody else's problem. The front lines of literacy in Alabama and around the world seem endless, and there's both a place and a great need for you on those front lines. There's room for you to work with another brother or sister, an adult or child, who wants to learn to read to unlock the mysteries and opportunities of words and to create a brighter and more fulfilling tomorrow.

Illiteracy is not an unsolvable problem, as countries like Cuba, Costa Rica and others have demonstrated (Cleckler, 2008). It doesn't require massive buildings or new institutions; you can teach someone to read with a newspaper, book or magazine. But it does require some financial support and, even more, time and human capital—people who can read, people who care, people who commit to helping others learn to read. Maybe that's the only solution in our country to this stubborn and growing problem: We must fight it locally at the ground level with passionate people who engage on the front lines. We must fight it in the streets in our neighborhoods and communities—one tutor and one adult learner working together to bring to life the dream of reading: one person helping another person, or groups of people working together, lesson by lesson, week by week, in a supportive environment.

I'm sure this approach sounds impossible to some. After all, we are talking about 40 million Americans, and more every year that are functionally illiterate. But if you think it's impossible, I urge you to reflect for a few moments on the great-untapped potential to defeat illiteracy that now lies largely dormant in this country. I am referring to the millions of retirees who possess reading skills and have time to tutor, the millions of university students who have energy and passion for service work, and the millions of churchgoers and members of civic and social groups who want to make a positive difference in their communities. I believe the "impossible" is rich with possibilities.

I want to thank three literacy service providers who encouraged me throughout this process, shared their insights and suggestions and graciously connected me with many of the individuals who shared their stories in the book: Julia Chancy at Shelton State Community College in Tuscaloosa, Dave Holt at the Bessemer Public Library and Steve Hannum at the Literacy Council in Birmingham. Their passion for fighting illiteracy is infectious, and their personal stories of involvement are included in the book.

Finally, I want to thank the more than 2,000 students at the University of Alabama who in the past four years joined the advocacy group, Literacy is the Edge (LITE), and subsequently became reading and math tutors for hundreds of adults and children, or assistants for English as a Second Language programs, in the Tuscaloosa community. The enthusiasm and spirit they bring to the cause of literacy continues to be a great source of inspiration for me and for members of the Literacy Council of West Alabama.

So much of my life has involved reading and using words that I can't imagine not being able to read. I hope the stories of these 30 heroic individuals on the front lines of literacy move you to action in your community. After all, what finer thing can anyone do than positively influence the life of another?

— Bruce K. Berger

Stories of Redemption

Living on the edge

1. Learning give me courage

The story of **Odella Williams,** adult learner, Birmingham

I was born in Americus, Georgia, a little place not even on a map. I was adopted and taken to Florida where I was raised. Back in those days, the schools wasn't segregated. They wasn't teaching us very much, but they passing us anyway. I remember going to the teacher once, telling her I couldn't read very well, I couldn't spell. But she was doing her nails, you know? She say, "Just go away, girl, go sit back down." That's the way my schooling went. I grew up with not much education, and I dropped out when I was 13.

I also run away from home at 13 because my father was abusive to me and my mother. First time I run away, I went straight to the juvy home. But they called my father, and he come and took me back home. So I just run away again. I never looked back. I ended up on this lady's porch, wrapped up in a blanket, sleeping on a chair. She came out and goes, "Honey, who are you? Are you hungry?" I told her, "Yes, I'm hungry." She took me under her wing for awhile. I did some chores and stuff, and she kept me. She was a nice lady.

But I got bored and left, and that's when I got into another kind of lifestyle. You know what I'm saying? I became a prostitute. I never tried to go back to school. I got really messed up for a long time, and now I'm 49. Can you believe it? I went through a lot. And I finally come to a time after I was in and out of jail so many times, I just got tired of it, you know? But when I decided to change, I realized I didn't have no real education, so what would I do? I couldn't go back to school, but then I found my tutor here, this lady in Birmingham, and she help me. She take her time and she so patient. You feel comfortable. She coaches you. Don't just tell you what to do, but *how* to do. I know I got to go back to where I left off at age 13 to catch up. But with people like Miss Tommie, I think I can do it. I know I can. I'm going to make it.

I got so many things I want to do now since I changed my lifestyle. I want to tackle the world, you know? And I figure if I learn how to read better, then I can do just about anything. My goal right now is improve my reading and get my GED. Then I'm going to pick me a trade and make a career. Maybe open up a big recovery place because I want to help someone. I want to give back, you know? I want to do something I know about, and I sure know recovery from my own experiences. I know what people need to help them recover. I been there more than once.

If I could spell real good, I'd write a book. I'd encourage others with my writing, I know I could. I've written my life story. I have it at home. I read it a lot to remind me of life then and now. Someday I'm going to write my story for others. I want to shine in a good way to help people. We all need some help, don't you think?

> **170,000 adults in Jefferson County, Alabama, read below a fifth-grade level.**
>
> — *M-POWER Ministries, Birmingham*

Kind of life I was in, I never really had a role model. I mostly had to shape my own life. And I was living in the fast lane, making money, making lots of money, so much money, and it was hard to let it go. I met a lot of people those years, and they had a lot of money, too. Now it's a whole different thing. Now there's no money, there's just struggle—*but*, I ain't got to live like I used to, I know that. I know I can still make some money, but I just got to go by another way to do it. I started out on my own at the age of 13, so I just had to survive. You know what I'm saying?

When I was in my early 20s, I was in a relationship with a man, and I left him. Now, he didn't want me to. He so mad, he put a contract out on me, you know? And I was beat. I was beat until I practically dead, paralyzed for nearly five years. The blows to my head was so extreme my doctors said they don't know how I survived it. I stayed in the hospital for a long time. Today I just feel so blessed because I can walk again. I been given another chance. And I want to try to do something with my life. Not having much schooling, they wanted to label me brain damaged from the beating, but I fought against that. I'm not damaged that way. I just need some more education, some help.

When I got a little bit better and away from the life I was on—drugs like cocaine, crack, you name it— when I got a little bit better, I started to feel blessed. So many people just don't make it back, you know? But I believed I was on the way back. I was face-to-face with all kinds of stuff, and I think today, with this much of my mind left, it's a great thing. And I want to use it. I'm preparing myself. With God and me together, I can do this. I'm inspired to do this.

I don't want to work at McDonald's for the rest of my life. Nothing against McDonald's, it's a job after all, and I'm thankful for that. But I can't see myself doing that for the rest of my life. I'm going to reach higher. I'm going to reach all the way up. When I tell people

my goal, they say, "Girl, you got a long ways to go."
And I say, "Okay, but I'm not mad about it. Are you?"

Miss Tommie helping me to read, spell, do math.
She help me to pay attention to what I'm doing. You
know what I'm saying? She's teaching me, do the
things I need to do to accomplish what I want to do.
That's a great gift. She's preparing me so I can go and
get my GED. She's brought my reading level up higher,
my spelling is better. I still got a ways to go, but I'm
moving ahead now.

Reading and filling out forms, that's easier. Some of
the words are still difficult, but now I know how to
think about them and attack them to get the meaning.
I didn't know how before. I'm going to get me a little
dictionary. Sometimes, maybe you don't know the
word, but if you have a dictionary, and if you look up
the word, sometimes you can figure it out by reading
the meaning of it. Breaking them down into syllables
helps, too.

Learning give me courage. Yes, I still got things to
work on, but I got more courage now. It's not an easy
road, but it's not a bad road either. You know what I'm
saying? You got to go out and work, do some footwork
to get faster and go further. You got to want it and be
willing to work for it. That's all. That's a big learning
for me. I'm excited about it. I can't wait to see what the
future holds.

What I learned is you need to read a little every
day. When you waiting somewhere, read a little. When
you riding in the car, read a little. Read a little every
day. Someday, you will read a lot, and you know
suddenly where you been, where you at.

I know some people are too embarrassed to ask for
help. Or they feel degraded because they don't have

education. And they probably been called *illiterate*. What I say to them is, "Forget all that. This is for you, honey. This about you, not them. You don't have to feel that way. You can do it. I can do it. We can do it."

2. Highs, lows and saving lives

The story of **Neil Segars,** teacher and tutor, Donaldson Correctional Facility, Bessemer

FIVE years ago I volunteered to design and teach an accelerated learning course at Donaldson Correctional Facility, a maximum security prison near Bessemer. The class helps inmates develop learning techniques, build confidence, improve their reading skills and prepare for the GED. This work has confirmed my belief that education and reading enrich lives and even save them. Along the way to Donaldson, my own life, my faith and my work have undergone extreme highs and horrible lows, and I want to tell you my story.

I was born in Birmingham on the west side of town between two steel mills—the Fairfield Mill and the Ensley Mill. I graduated from the University of Alabama in Tuscaloosa and earned an engineering degree in 1961. I took a job with Deering Milliken in South Carolina, and then returned to Birmingham as an engineer with St. Regis Paper Company. I attended law school at nights, graduated, and completed the bar exam in 1968. By that time I was in the computer business with Sperry Univac.

In 1970 my wife and I moved to Cincinnati, where I was area manager for the company for the next seven years. I went to Xavier University during this period and earned an M.B.A. We came back to Birmingham in 1978 with our four children, and I opened my own company, MidSouth Data Industries. It was a systems integration company that grew to 70 employees and

Motivated by his faith and personal tribulations, Neil Segars has focused on teaching inmates not just how to read and write but how to learn.

offices in five states over the next 20 years, and I have wonderful memories of our success and the good times we had. But it was also during this time that my wife and I began raising our two granddaughters. The youngest was born addicted to drugs, and we brought her home from the neonatal intensive care unit and soon had her four-year-old sister also. All this was done through the Jefferson County Family Courts.

I grew up in the Baptist Church and always wanted to be more spiritual than I was. It bothered me that I did not have a relationship to Jesus Christ. Then I was invited to go on the Emmaus Walk one weekend, a powerful experience that is sponsored by the Methodist Church. I had read in the Bible that Jesus encountered a man whose son fell down and frothed at the mouth, possessed by a demon. The father said to Jesus, *Can you heal him?* And Jesus said, *I can, if you believe I can.* And the man said, *I believe, Lord, but help me with my unbelief.* I was quite struck by that because that was me all over—my unbelief.

I went to the chapel early one morning that weekend and was sitting and praying when this incredible vision came to me. Jesus Christ was standing there, and this is the absolute truth, he was standing there and he said to me: *Let not your heart be troubled. You believe in God; believe also in me.* This was what Jesus had said in John 14:1. That seared me to the core, and I came away from that chapel a completely changed man in my relationship to the Lord. I knew that I got it. I understood. When I came home that Sunday evening, my wife said, what's wrong with you? You're glowing. That was the beginning of my being deeply spiritual and my journey to the prison.

When you complete an Emmaus Walk, they encourage you to join an accountability group, so I did. The group I joined went out to the Donaldson Correctional Facility on a regular basis with the Kairos Prison Ministry. Kairos means *God's special time or timing* in Greek, and is similar in structure to an Emmaus Walk. In 1993, I went into the general population at Donaldson for the first time for a Kairos weekend. My first day there, we're sitting around a table and introducing ourselves, and I turned to the man on the right and said, my name is Neil Segars. Now, this man is a huge, mountain of a man, and he said to me, my name is Doc and I'm a psychopathic killer. I said, well Doc, I'm so glad to meet you, and I'm looking forward to spending the weekend with you. I was lying through my teeth, but he was just testing me. We actually became close friends, and it was that experience and those miracles I've seen in the prison ever since that weekend that have kept me going back to the prison for Kairos.

In 1995, we were allowed to go onto death row for the first time. There are 24 cells on death row, and we took the Kairos program there. One of the things that keeps me going back, and I've seen it with my own eyes, is that some men on death row *are* converted; they have complete changes in their heart, attitude and lives. I've seen men in the general population who committed bad crimes but then completed their time and became good people, solid citizens on the outside.

One man on death row was like that, Billy Wayne Waldrop. He was a horrible inmate until he came to know the Lord. In prison he eventually became an ordained minister through a mail-order program. Billy became a role model for others in prison. He helped bring other men to Christ. So when Billy Wayne received his execution orders, a number of us in the prison ministry and the Kairos program went to the governor and tried to stop that execution. But his life ended in January 1997.

My own life was about to head into a steep dive, too. With the prison work, my church work, my involvement in a growing business, and some serious family and legal issues with a daughter whose children we were raising, I woke up one morning in March of 1997 and couldn't get out of bed. I mean I was com-

> **Seventy percent of inmates in federal and state prisons are functionally illiterate or read below the eighth-grade level.**
>
> — *Karl Haigler,*
> *Literacy Behind*
> *Prison Walls*

pletely locked up—mentally, physically, every other way. That rubber band I'd become was stretched so tight that it just snapped overnight. I literally couldn't get out of bed. I didn't want to do anything. I didn't want to shave. I wanted no external stimuli, no television or radio. I just wanted to sit alone in a corner and be quiet. I was totally paralyzed by depression.

I went back to work, but I wasn't the same person. I'd walk into my office, give everyone a big hello, then say that I had some things to do, and go into my office, close the door and lie down on the floor. That was how I operated for some time. I went to see a psychiatrist, and then another one and another one, but I didn't get any better. That was my life; the depression was overwhelming.

Over the next few years, things went from bad to worse and then to the bottom. The year 2000 was the perfect storm with Y2K. Companies spent so much money to prepare for that. The dot.com marketplace imploded, and the stock market went south. Large companies were getting heavy into data communications, and since I had the most experienced engineers in this field in the Southeast, those companies raided me of my best engineers. They paid them double what I could. So Y2K and its expenses, the collapse of dot.com companies and the fall of the market, and the loss of my top 7-8 engineers caused me to file corporate bankruptcy in July of 2000.

The next week my wife had a physical exam, and they discovered a lump in her breast and she underwent a radical mastectomy. So there we were: My wife was very ill, I had severe depression and a bankrupt business, we were raising two little girls and then I had to file for personal bankruptcy. Since I had had to personally guarantee payments of the loans to my company when it went bankrupt, the banks came after me for payment. They came after everything—our house, car, all of our assets. We almost lost it all.

That was the absolute lowest point of my life, and I could only see one way out. So I started home one day not long after the bankruptcy and drove to my son's house. I knew where he kept his firearms, and that's what I wanted. I went into the closet and pulled down the box with the firearms. I sat on the edge of the bed and pulled a Glock pistol out of the box. I took a clip and popped it into the pistol. Then I set the pistol beside me on the bed and sat thinking for a time. I knew what I wanted to do, but when I reached for the pistol, an amazing thing happened. I heard two little female voices saying over and over, *Papa don't do it. Don't do it, papa.* The voices sounded just like my two beautiful little granddaughters. That brought me to my senses, and I removed the clip and put everything away. As I walked down the steps of the house, I said, *Lord, I am nothing but a shell of a man. Do with me whatever you want to do.*

> **Eighty-five percent of juveniles who come before the courts are functionally illiterate.**
>
> — *Jonathan Kozol*
> *Illiterate America*

Two weeks later, after changing psychiatrists again, I went to the new doctor and he thought I should try a new medication. I started the new medication that afternoon, and I'm going to tell you, the black clouds rolled away! Those dark clouds of hopelessness just up and rolled away in that spring of 2001. My mind cleared, and I have not looked back since. It is unbelievable the difference that medication has made for me. We are electrochemical animals, and I guess if that gets out of balance, we are in trouble. Finally, I began to think straight again.

During all of this, I continued doing the Kairos weekends at the prison. It was so important to me, and I began to notice the men in the prison were like some of the young boys in my elementary school: They couldn't sit still in class. They weren't unteachable, but they got that label because of their behavior. I also remembered my own experience in law school: I worked during the day and went to school at night, and I was exhausted. I read and reread pages and cases and couldn't remember anything. I was sure I would never make it. I went to the public library to find some help for my concentration and memory problems in law school, and I found the most incredible book by Harry Lorayne, *How to Develop a Super Power Memory*.

The book was so good it got me completely through law school. I also was reminded of the power of learning by doing, by using my hands. I had a friend who taught me to tune my own car. Now, I could have read about how to do it, or sat in a class and had somebody tell me how to do it, and probably still couldn't have done it. But by having a friend talk me through the tune-up process while I actually did it was a great form of learning for me. The learning went from my fingers to my brain and stayed there. I thought about the different learning styles that people have. Some learn primarily through their eyes, some through their ears, and some through their hands or fingers, by doing.

So I asked the prison chaplain if he'd let me develop a course for the inmates. I wanted to call it "accelerated learning" to help the inmates learn how to learn—to give them the same kind of confidence I had found, that they could learn anything. I taught the first class in January through October, 2006. The first step is to survey and test the class to determine their predominant learning style. Most of the men came to realize that they learned primarily through their fingers, not their ears, as in a lecture class.

Then I taught them memory techniques and associations like I had discovered in Harry Lorayne's book. And it worked: They were amazed by what they could learn and remember. From there, I went into reading. We'd work on comprehension, understanding and speed. As a part of this section, I'd have them read books like *To Kill a Mockingbird, Call of the Wild* or *Shane*, and they liked them. I first have them read the book. Then I'd rent or buy a DVD, and we'd view that and discuss the book versus the movie—what they read, what they saw, what they thought.

The next step involved teaching sections on contracts and on torts, personal injuries, that type of thing. Both of them are very important in today's world, and this section takes about three months to complete. We'd use what we learned and then examine case studies, which they understood very quickly. I show the movie *Twelve Angry Men,* which does a remarkable job illustrating the inner workings of a jury.

Then we spend several weeks on computer simulations, learning virtually. This is a very effective way for learning battlefield planning, cockpit simulation for airline pilots, or operation simulation for medical students and doctors, and so forth. So I take my laptop computer into the prison loaded with software. I use Microsoft Flight Simulator. The men literally sit in the cockpit, hands on a control stick and throttle, where they can see the instruments and do an actual simulated take off and landing. So they experience what it feels like to take off and land an airplane through computer simulation. They really enjoy this hands-on part of the class. I also teach them how to use Microsoft Word to write a simple letter, and Excel to do basic calculations.

It takes about a year to complete the course, and then we hold a small graduation ceremony. I'm allowed to bring in Cokes, cookies and peanuts, and I hand out a nice certificate of completion to them. I give them four copies so they can put one in their file, or their jacket as they call it, and send one to momma, or a girlfriend, or whomever to let them know what they accomplished. Typically, I have 20-25 in the class. The biggest takeaway is that they now feel that they can learn just about anything. They seem to gain tremendous learning confidence. They come to believe and know that they can read, understand and learn.

So my life has had some serious highs and lows, but my faith and my focus on education and spiritual outreach have sustained me. I'm now supplementing my work in prison education with adult tutoring in the community. I want to teach in the community here and encourage those who need help to get help. I think you need to do that face-to-face. Learning to read opens so many doors ... for people in our communities, and even for men and women in prison. Reading enriches lives, and I've also learned it helps save them.

3. A good day

The story of **Tiffany Foreman**, University of Alabama student and adult tutor, Tuscaloosa

A serious car accident three years ago profoundly re-shaped who I am and what's important in my life. Before the accident I was a student at the University of Alabama, and I partied all the time—drinking, drugs, everything a student shouldn't do. Then after some heavy drinking one night, I drove a friend's car too fast, it went out of control and it flipped over nine times. I broke my neck and was in the hospital for two months. I don't remember any part of the wreck, or anything that happened for a month after the accident. That month just disappeared somewhere in my memory.

My mom took care of me for a year. I couldn't go to school. I couldn't go to work. I was in bed and in every kind of rehab you can imagine for most of a year. I know I was pretty terrible to my mom before the accident. We didn't spend much time together. But afterward she took off work to stay with me 24/7. I was literally helpless for months. I had a neck brace and two casts on my arms, and I couldn't bathe myself, so she did that. We spent a lot of time together. Now I call her at least once a day and often more. We're very close. Regardless of how many times I screwed up, how many times I pushed her away before, she still did everything for me, she was there for me when nobody else was, and she took care of me, financially and physically.

The doctors told me that if I had another accident I probably wouldn't survive it. In fact, I suffered a major head injury in the accident, and I technically have a learning disability as a result. So I've changed in about every way. I don't drink anymore. I don't do drugs. I don't party. It's safe to say that I really don't do much of anything wrong anymore.

Eventually I returned to school, and I became involved in tutoring through a special education class. One of the class requirements was to volunteer in the community. The options for volunteering were all with children, except for the opportunity to tutor an adult through the PLUS program at Shelton State. So I did that. I went through about three hours of training with the books and programs. Now I'm an adult reading tutor, and I talk to the program advisor, Miss Julia Chancy, at least once a week and let her know how things are going.

> **Only 35 percent of the least literate American adults are fully employed.**
>
> — *David Baldacci*

My adult student—I'll call her Lindy—and I write Miss Chancy letters every time we finish a lesson and tell her how Lindy is doing. Lindy is extremely compassionate toward everyone. At the end of our first session together, she was so appreciative that she told me she loved me. She's just a precious individual. I met with her 2-3 times a week during the fall, and this spring we are working together once a week. We've worked together for about eight months now. Her goal is to get a job with a cleaning crew that comes through the building she lives in. She didn't get a job with them earlier, though she tried. So she wants to improve enough to gain a job like that.

After a debilitating automobile accident totally upended her life, Tiffany Foreman turned to tutoring to meet a class requirement. She found she loved it. Now, she not only helps her student, Lindy, but Lindy's whole family.

Lindy's a year younger than I, and she has a severe learning disability. Miss Chancy told me that it was an inherited problem. But she and her parents are fantastic. They all call me frequently. Her mom asks me for help with things on my computer. Her dad calls to get advice about purchase decisions. For example, recently they've seen some things on TV advertised at supposedly low prices, let's say $200. And her dad may think that's a great price, but I explain to him if he will wait a few months, he can probably buy it in a store for $30. I tell him just to wait.

One approach I use a lot with Lindy is to have her make index cards with new words on them; I'm faithful about doing that so she can study and practice with them. One time she was having difficulty with the "a-r" sounds. For example, the letter "r" and the word "are" sound just the same, and she was confused by that. So we made a special grouping of cards with words with the "r" sound, and she studied them. The next time I met with her, she knew them all!

That was a big day for her, so we went to Dip 'n Dots for ice cream to celebrate. There's a nice girl who works there, and she lets you sample every kind of taste, if you want, and Lindy and her mom tried about 10 different kinds before they selected one. Usually, I give her something useful when she's making progress, like highlighters or cute pens or pencils. One time she saw that I had an eraser topper on one of my pencils, and she liked that. So I took her a pack of those the next time I met with her.

We meet at the Tuscaloosa Public Library, and I think our sessions mean a lot to Lindy. She calls it "school" when we meet, and she's always excited and comes with a little backpack of things—pencils, highlighters, study books—just like someone going to school. Sometimes she talks about going to school forever, but I tell her that I will eventually get a job somewhere else, and she might, too.

I honestly became a tutor just to fulfill a class requirement, but I've continued to tutor because I like Lindy, and the sessions have come to mean a great deal to me personally. I started to feel that I was actually doing something good, I was helping someone else. That felt good. As far as my own education and going to school, I know that I'm benefiting myself, too. I'm making my life better. I understand that. But being with Lindy, I'm also helping her, and I truly enjoy being with her.

I had a "lightbulb experience" several weeks ago. I was having difficulties in my own studies. It seemed to take a lot of reading for me to understand and comprehend my own assignments. I was so concerned I even met with some of my teachers. But by the following Monday, when I went to see Lindy, I actually felt like I knew what I was doing. In fact, in working through my own difficulties, I figured out how to help Lindy get through some reading difficulties she was having. That was a good day!

I think that class service requirements are a great way to get more college students involved in fighting illiteracy. The class forces them to participate, and once that happens, some of them will stay involved. They may even become tutors for life, or volunteer for other causes in their communities.

4. Strength for just another minute

The story of **Robert Marlowe,** adult tutor, Bessemer

I was born in Hollywood, Florida, but grew up in Tuscaloosa. I came to Bessemer for a program at the Foundry Rescue and Mission Recovery Center to deal with a drug addiction that's been ongoing since I was about 13 years old. I'm 26 now. So I come up here and got treatment and eventually graduated from a 12-month program.

I met Dave Holt here at the library, and he asked me if I was interested in tutoring for him. I took it on about five months ago and began tutoring a 13-year-old boy. He was already a pretty good reader, and I believe I've learned more from him than he has from me. He's got a little attention deficit disorder, and it's hard for him to sit still. He reminds me an awful lot of myself when I was young and growing up. It's been uplifting for me to be able to help somebody in need, and to get outside of myself and actually be doing some of the things that Jesus wants us to do here on earth.

I got saved when I was eight years old, but then I rebelled and run away from the Lord for years. It's real hard for me to pick through my past and find very many good things that happened, apart from getting my GED and going to college. I went for one quarter at Shelton State, and it was hard. I wasn't totally committed to or interested in education or college, so I guess it didn't really impact my life. I got my GED when I was at Mt. Megs, which is a juvenile facility. But the rest of it, I don't know.

As a child when I was growing up, amongst drugs, alcohol, and other things in the house I was raised in Tuscaloosa, I had an uncle who lived down the way. He was a Christian who lived a moral life and from time to time he'd take me to church. He kind of set that standard in my life, planted the seed as to what was right. And this kind of followed me throughout life, all the years of trouble I went through.

So, from eight years old I always knew of God and who the Lord was, and knew what was right, but I just never had the strength or the self-control to live out a moral life. I was just rebellious and disobedient in general, and it took losing everything, burning bridges with family members and friends, and finding myself broke and sent back to the county jail to finally realize that my life's not going nowhere. I was stuck forever, it seemed, in a cycle of meth, cocaine and crack addiction, just a constant circle, and I finally called on the Lord again, and he helped me.

I'm not sure exactly what it was, but something happened then that got me fully committed to him. I found the strength to live a life of more control and morality. It's still a struggle sometimes. But I believe God is sovereign, I believe in Jesus Christ, and that he come and died for our sins. I truly believe that the only way we can live and make it in this life, and live a good and a real righteous life, is in and through him. That don't mean we're not going to have struggles and downfalls, or be perfect people. I believe we live in a world that has fallen, and daily it falls a bit more.

So it's still a struggle, but I believe it's going to be very worth it in the end. God's the real ultimatum in my life right now because I can't find the strength within myself to make it any other way. I've proven that time and time again. I can't really explain the strength he gives me; it's just a change in mindset and in my heart. It's not really about feelings and emotions changing, but sometimes it might be just strength to go on for another day. Sometimes strength for just another minute, you know?

My cousin, Billy, he's a recovering drug addict, clean now for maybe 15 or 16 years. He became hooked on crack cocaine when he was 18 years old. He helped shape my life and has been a real role model for me in terms of how you can overcome drug addiction and move on and have a better life. He ended up moving to Georgia, got a college degree, became an X-ray technician. He's married, has a kid and is making good money. He's living a straight life and he knows God and he prays. He's been a real encouragement to me. I lived with him when I was younger, and he's always been there to talk with me and lift me up.

> **The 2003 National Assessment of Adult Literacy (NAAL) indicated that 11 million U.S. adults are non-literate in English, and 30 million U.S. adults read below the basic level; they are functionally illiterate.**
>
> — *ProLiteracy, 2006*

My uncle Ron used to carry me to church when I was real young. He's been there to talk to me and guide me. He's retired from a BF Goodrich tire plant, and now he's a song director at a church. And Dave Holt here, and a lot of people at the Foundry—they've all had a big impact on my life. But Dave and Pastor Allen over at Pleasant Hill Church, they are two regular guys who took the time to help somebody out and give me some faith and hope.

Tutoring is something different for me. I couldn't have seen it coming five years ago, but it's been a great experience. It's probably been a more important experience for me than the teenager I'm tutoring. It's helped me a lot to be able to work with somebody, use a few leadership skills. We've been working together for about five months.

This young man, he's already a pretty good reader. He sometimes has a hard time pronouncing words, breaking them down, but he's a good reader. Focus is somewhat difficult for him, and sitting still, so I try to help him focus, figure out the word, keep his attention. I'm learning patience. I've shared just a little of my life story with him, some things I've been through. Sometimes we pray together. He wants to read the Bible, so sometimes we read out of the Bible together.

What I take away from this experience is some leadership—being able to work with youth. I hope I can be a testament as to what they can accomplish. But most of all, I take away being able to help somebody in need a little bit. That feels good to me; it feels right. It's real important for me to get out of my comfort zone, to help. I'm gaining patience, too. I guess another thing is the one-on-one relationship time. My relationships in the past have faltered in that area. So this helps me.

I don't know if I'll do more of this in the future. If the Lord leads me into it, yes. Maybe on another level, maybe working with youth. Maybe he's preparing me to work with youth on a different level. Sometimes I feel burnt out at the end of our hour together. It's hard for me to sit still, too. I can just imagine how he feels. Honestly, that's a 50-50 proposition about the future. I can see myself working with youth, maybe with kids in the church.

I just got back from a mission trip to Biloxi, Mississippi and that was really exciting. We helped some people restore their homes; they're still recovering from Hurricane Katrina. A group of 15 of us from Pleasant Hill Church went there for three days, and we got to do drywall, tile work, things like that. I've worked in construction a lot, so I could use my skills and feel good about that. I think I'm doing God's will, and I'm definitely interested in more missionary work. I felt real good being there and working. I used to live in Gulfport, Mississippi so it was in the neighborhood. I've got a longing to be near the coast, so maybe I'll get me a house down there someday. Maybe I'll get to travel more. I always wanted to do that. Maybe things are starting to fall into place for me.

Longer term, I want to go back to school, but right now I don't feel I'm quite stable enough to do that. I don't want to commit to something that I might not be able to complete, but maybe later I can handle it. I think I'd like to study and get a degree in ministry. Who knows what the Lord has planned for me? Longer term I'd like to get my own place, a car, and live the old square John life. That sounds pretty good to me.

We make a six-month commitment to tutor. It's not that hard to find a little time to help someone. Even if it doesn't seem like you're making progress, you actually are. There will come a time in their life when, if you really open yourself and your heart up to that student, they're going to remember it. It will impact them in some way, in a good way, I think. That personal connection and bond is what counts. Touching heart to heart, not just on a reading level but a personal level, that means a lot to both of you.

5. Cheating my own life

The story of **Kimberly Burrell,** adult learner, Birmingham

GROWING up I didn't have anyone to push me in terms of education. My grandmother did the best she could, but she didn't know how to read. I was rebellious and always mad because my parents had just dumped me off with my grandmother. I was the second of nine children in my family, and my parents weren't able to keep the four oldest children, so my brother and I ended up with our grandmother. Learning was not one of my highest priorities. I'd go to school and get into trouble. As an adult, I just kind of hid it, you know? I wouldn't tell people I couldn't read, or that I needed help. I was angry all of the time, and I ended up hooked on alcohol and drugs just like my parents had been hooked.

But at the end of this month, it will make one year that I've been clean from drugs and alcohol. So in doing that and coming into this reading program, I decided I wasn't going to continue wearing that mask and hiding it. I'd make up excuses and say I can't see the words, or I wear glasses and forgot them, just any old excuse to keep from reading, and having to admit I couldn't. But no more.

I've been coming here since November of 2009. I'm excited about it because my reading is getting a lot better. My comfort zone is better. I'm not as angry as I was. Now it's like a whole different world has opened up. Before when I looked at a newspaper, all I saw is all of those letters running together, and I didn't know what they meant and it was frustrating. But Miss Tommie has taught me how to "look for the word inside the word," like she say, and it's helped. I feel better about myself. Learning how to read has bettered my self-esteem, so I'm excited about it.

Miss Tommie is a wonderful teacher. She has so much patience. I remember the first day I came in they give you a little test of words to see where your reading is. I was just really frustrated and didn't think I did that good. But Miss Tommie said, "Actually, you did better and you are better than you think you are." Well, how about that!

I started out on a grade one level, and then she skipped me to grade three level. So I must have learned a few things in school. I'm working in grade three now, and I'm excited about it. I try to come here to work on my reading five days a week. This is my priority, and I treat it like I would treat a job—five days a week for 2-6 hours each day. We have these little quick books that we get to read, and one day I was in class and I finished a whole book in six hours. It was like, the more I could read, the more I wanted to read. It was like opening up something that just keeps on opening up more, you know? What they say—peeling an onion?

I want to get my reading up to par to allow me to try to get my GED. I was always one of those people never completed anything. I think I was afraid of success, or afraid people would learn I couldn't read, so I'd pretend and hide behind stuff. Now I'm aiming to get my GED. With that and the street knowledge I have, I hope to be a counselor and help people hooked on drugs. If I can reach that goal before I turn 55, I think I've beat it.

The thing that's really important to me now is my volunteer work with AIDS Alabama. I'm a peer counselor, and when people come in, I test them. If they test positive, then I put them in touch with a caseworker who helps them find housing, medicine, food and things. If you can help one person, it makes a big difference. When I first started there, I couldn't read the questionnaires to people, but now I can sit there and read the questions on the form and get feedback from the patients.

One in seven adults in the U.S. lacks the literacy skills required to read anything more complex than a children's book, a staggering statistic that has not improved in more than 10 years.

— *Jessica Calefati, U.S. News & World Report, 2009*

Reading also has made my self-esteem a lot better. I'm starting to believe there isn't anything I can't do. My confidence is growing. I always heard that you had to be able to read to get ahead in life, and now I know what they mean. I was cheating my own life before. It was like a piece of the puzzle was missing, and then somebody gave me that piece and made the puzzle whole.

I had two sons. I say "had" because my baby son was murdered seven years ago on the street. What I learned from him and that experience is that you have to live your life like it always the last day. If you can do something to help somebody, you should do it. Tomorrow is promised to nobody. I've been selfish, I know that. My life was all about me before, what I wanted, and what I wanted to do. But more and more now, I find my happiness in others.

My youngest son who died, he was so carefree and he inspired me to not hold back on life. My oldest son, who's 28, he's inspired me, too. Despite my battles with drugs and alcohol, he graduated from high school and went to college a few years. He has his own landscape business now, and he's a really hard worker. What he's given me is the determination to not quit—to hang on and keep after it.

I was diagnosed as HIV positive about 14 years ago, and my first thought was to walk out in front of a big truck and take my life. What was there to live for, you know? But in becoming clean and sober, and getting involved with AIDS Alabama, I don't see it now as a death sentence. I can live, I can help others, and I can go out and talk to kids at school. Nobody told me when I was a teenager, so I try to reach out. If I can reach somebody with my story, even one person, maybe they won't have to go through what I did. Maybe I can do something positive.

Reading makes a lot of differences in my daily life. I can go to the grocery store and actually read the labels on food cans and boxes. This might sound funny, but I used to go by what the pictures told me about what's inside the can. Imagine not reading labels. Now I can read them. Is it light and low in sodium? Does it have protein? Does it have honey wheat? I can now read what I'm putting in my body.

Reading also helped me with those GPS things, you know? When I go to AIDS conventions, I ride with a friend who has a GPS system, and before I started studying here, he would tell me to enter information in the GPS, but I couldn't. I couldn't spell the words. I couldn't connect the sounds with letters. But now I can. So it's opened a lot of doors for me, and that's why I'm excited.

Like other adults, I was afraid to trust at first. I never had anybody help me read. So when I first came and Miss Tommie handed me a book and asked me to read, wow! There was a lot of fear. I didn't want to be laughed at. The fear blocked me, but now I'm more confident. They don't laugh at me here. Miss Tommie makes it really easy, and if I can't read a word, or see the word in the word, she says just write it down. Then she ask, what word do you see, or take this part off and what do you see? I trust her.

It's a different world if you can trust, if you can improve your reading. You begin to look at life differently. Even though I was afraid, sometimes you have to be willing to take chances. I spent 47 years of my life not knowing how to read. In just a few months, coming here every day, I'm improving my reading. Nobody can take that from you. Before, if somebody handed me a piece of paper with words on it, that's what it was—a piece of paper with words. But today I can work with it, put some of the words together. It's like the light is coming on. It's slow, but the light is coming on. I wish there were reading programs like this everywhere.

Stories of Commitment

Leading the way

6. Recognizing the signs

The story of **Tommie Blanton,** adult tutor,
the Literacy Council in Birmingham

I had a wonderful childhood. My father passed away
when I was four, but what I can remember of him,
he was a loving and kind person. A lot of people liked
him. He was from Demopolis, Alabama, and at the
time I didn't know why so many people liked him, but
my mother phrased it like this: He was a root doctor.
He would go into the woods, and he knew all about
roots and things that would help people, and he would
gather the roots and mix them up, you know? If you
had a cold, he would cure your cold. If you had arthri-
tis, he had roots to help with that. So people would
come and get homemade remedies from him for so
many ailments.

My mother came from a very religious background.
Her father was a minister, and he helped organize a
church here in Birmingham. They really taught the
word and believe in the word. So I grew up in that type
of atmosphere. My mother made sure that we knew
the Bible, and she gave us some wonderful advice. To
this day I have remembered a lot of things she told us
and tried to share them with others—the love and
caring that God has given us. Do unto others, as you
would have them do unto you, she told us. Try to live
by the 10 commandments. She said it would be hard,
but try it anyway. Treat right each person you meet;
don't judge them, but check them out. Do not rush into judgment. She gave us advice like that, and that's
how I've tried to live.

My mother's brother was killed in the war, and at that time they gave the veteran's families $10,000 and his money went to my mother. She used that to build what I call the "home house." She made everyone welcome in the house, the women and their children. If you were a man, you had to work and get your own house. My mother was from Steen, Mississippi, and when others from Mississippi traveled to Birmingham, they were welcome to spend the night in the home house, even if they had to sleep on the floor, until they could get a job and move out on their own. So I got this giving and caring spirit from my mother, and I've tried to raise my children the same way.

I have four children who are biologically my own, and I adopted my oldest daughter's two children, so I have six in all. And I have eight grandchildren, one boy and seven girls. The youngest is four, and the oldest is 29. I like to enjoy my children and grandchildren. I used to like to travel a lot, but I don't do that much anymore. I go to church, enjoy a good quiet conversation, and sometimes dinner out or lunch out with friends. I like to be around interesting people and to learn. In April I'll be 70 years old, and I'm happy to still be here and contribute. As long as I have life, I want to continue to give what I can.

I went to school in Birmingham and then to Pontiac Community College in Michigan. I married a man who was in the Navy, and I travelled with him. I went to school wherever he was based. I wanted to be part of life, you know, and I knew that going to school and getting some education would help. I eventually got a job with the Birmingham Board of Education, and I worked with them for about 25 years.

I got into the literacy program about 10 or 11 years ago. My job then was to recruit volunteers—adults who could tutor. I trained them to become tutors. A lady on the Board of Education urged me to get involved. She felt I could be a valuable person in the literacy program in Birmingham. That's how I got involved in literacy, and I admire this woman because she was an influence on this part of my life. She had so much passion for the work. She told me that I could give my time and my understanding, and with my wisdom I could help and work with these people. I really like what we're doing here.

When I first started tutoring, I really didn't understand what literacy was all about. Let me tell you some stories to explain. I went over to the Adult Learning Center, and there was a parking lot there filled with so many cars that I asked a lady if these cars all belonged to people who were literacy students. Were there so many people looking for help? And she said, yes, they are. But they are driving beautiful cars, I said, and I didn't know what to think about that.

There was another student I saw in the grocery store one day, I guess she's about 45, and when I saw her she came over and asked me where something was, some food product. We were right there on the same

> **It requires ninth-grade competence to understand the antidote instructions on a bottle of corrosive kitchen lye, 10th-grade competence to understand instructions on a federal income tax return, 12th-grade competence to read a life insurance form.**
>
> — *Jonathan Kozol*
> *Illiterate America, p. 10*

aisle, and I didn't know she couldn't read, so I showed her what she was looking for. Then she asked me where something else was. And I realized then she couldn't read. So these things perked my interest, and I began learning how to recognize signs for people who can't read, and how they cope with everyday life. I never gave it much thought before. If you learned as a child how to read, you really don't think about how to survive if you can't read, or what the signs are for those who can't read. It really opened my eyes.

I discovered other signs, too: The way they talk sometimes; they are shy; they don't participate much in conversation; they will listen and let you talk; they're quiet, and if you ask their opinion, they don't give it too freely. But sometimes it's invisible. Sometimes they can speak well because they may be in a family or a circle where the language is used well. They listen to the news so they know what's going on, and they can talk about that. They may dress well. They may drive big cars.

There was a man at the Adult Learning Center who had a job and whose wife was a teacher. But he could not read. I didn't know that until he was assigned to me to work with. His wife read the newspaper to him every day. And if you met him, and talked with him, you would never know he couldn't read.

I had another experience when I was much younger. I was going to pay my neighbor's utility bills, and I saw people go up to the cashier to pay their bill. They would take the bill in one hand, and their money in another, and then just lay everything on the counter for the clerk, who would count out the money and give them their change. I eventually realized what was going on—they couldn't count their money and they couldn't read.

So I try to pay better attention now, and I try to encourage people who might need help. But I've learned that it is very, very difficult to help adults learn to read because there is so much you have to learn as a child between the ages of 4-8. If you don't get it there, if you don't understand the basics, it's very difficult as an adult to develop those skills. I work with several ladies now, they finished high school, but they can't read. They are in their 40s, but they didn't develop those skills as children, even though they went through the high school system. For example, there are some things I just can't seem to get over to them— simple words like did, that, them, is, and are, the "help me" words. It's the strangest thing because they can recognize big words better than the little words.

I'm working with two ladies now who don't have anyone at home to help them with their homework, so I'm trying to make sure they get tape recorders so we can tape the homework and the words they need to learn. Then we can put them on cards and go through them again and again. If they have tape recorders, they can master some of that.

One of the young ladies who comes here, for example, she takes the bus, and she was saying that some of the words she didn't recognize on the signs and things before, she knows them now. Another says she can do a little more reading than she could do in the beginning, and I can see that. Another young lady, she lives in a home per se, and she was saying that she can read and recognize some things. She's finished reading a book that she's worked on for a long time. She can recognize the words and knows them. I think she will

Tommie Blanton, who has tutored adult learners for more than a decade, suggests that success depends on making no assumptions. She spends time getting to know all her students and then continuously praises their progress.

master it. She tells me she now has confidence, where at one time she would not dare to pick up and try to read anything in front of others. They do have success stories, and I can appreciate that.

I think any community can do more to help with literacy. You can go into any community and start with a church. Ask the pastor if they would be willing to have a literacy class in the church, and spread the word from there. You also can visit the school board and see if they are willing to open the schools in the evening. You also have to have tutor-training classes, and you can do that with people in the church because you have teachers there, and doctors and lawyers, all kinds of people. Ask them if they would be willing to help. And then go out and talk to people in the community, let them know you are there, you care and help is available. It really starts by getting out there and talking to others in the community. You'd be surprised what falls on peoples' ears and into their hearts to get out and do something. I believe people in the church ought to be curious enough to find out if I can read, and then help me if I can't.

So you can go out into your church, or any group you are working with, and let them know about this opportunity. Give them some success stories. And if you talk about it enough, and if people are willing to help, then some of the people who never thought it could happen for them, they will begin to take the steps to make it happen for them. They will stop saying I can't and start saying, I can. And you've got to encourage them with those words. I always say come out of the closet into the light and try to see what you can do. Say I can, or I'm going to try.

Encouragement is a big part of the tutoring job. And you have to have wisdom. You also need to have a lot of Christ in your life, and you have to have a lot of patience and a lot of heart. Many illiterate people are ashamed to let anybody know; it's their big secret. So you have to keep encouraging them. And you will have to repeat things. And maybe you will have to change things up. When they get tired or discouraged, you must change or switch your approach. You come at it in a different way to get them back on track.

You also have to research each individual. You must look for other books and readings to make it interesting to them and keep them coming along. You have to greet them and make them feel good when they walk up to you, no matter how they are dressed or appear. If you don't, that's it; they will back off and won't try it again. So above all, you have to be caring for each individual.

And you must support them in other terribly important ways. You have to look for organizations that can help them. Sometimes they have problems just buying food, or paying their utility bills. They may be living on the street. So you have to locate some place or organization where they can receive help. You have to help them with their lives.

When you tutor and help someone learn to read, you also become part of their lives, and you have to help them with their lives. When you do, they come to believe that life is worth living. That's what I've learned in experiences with my students.

7. Reading's about a future, isn't it?

The story of **Joyce Binion,** adult tutor and retired teacher, Bessemer

I was born here and went to McAdory School in McCalla, the same school my parents attended many years ago. I graduated from the University of Alabama with a degree in elementary education. Then I went to Montgomery and taught second graders and sixth graders. That's where I met my husband; he was the band director at Sidney Lanier High School. He was very successful, and his bands won many competitions and once travelled to Disney World in California to perform.

We moved from Montgomery to the University of Texas at Austin, where my husband worked on his graduate studies. Then we moved to Victoria, Texas, where I taught remedial reading for two years in a very mixed system—one-third Hispanic, one-third White, one-third Black. That was a challenging but fun experience. All the students could speak English, but reading and comprehension were difficult so we worked together in class to improve. Then we moved back to Phenix City in Alabama where I taught and eventually retired from teaching after 33 years. My husband died from cancer. Our son attended the University of Alabama where he was the drum major. Today he's a band director in Chilton County.

I became involved in tutoring through my church— Pleasant Hill United Methodist. We started a GED program, in conjunction with Lawson State, where students could come to our church and develop their reading skills. I got involved with that program, but we couldn't keep the attendance numbers up so the program closed. Then Dave Holt said they could use some help with the reading program here at the library in Bessemer, so I became involved.

I had been taking care of my parents—one was 95 and one was 96. They died this past year, and so for the first time really in my life, I had no obligations. There was time for other things, I needed something to do, and I've been at it for eight or nine months. Kayla is my student now.

My parents were my role models. My father had a dairy—a hard physical job—and he worked long hours to be successful. He was a member of the Alabama Farmer's Federation. When he retired, he sold the dairy property to Bent Brook Golf Course, which kept the house and barns for workers to live in while they were building the golf course. Then they tore everything down except the silo, which still triggers childhood memories when I see it.

> **America's workforce is compromised by a lagging K-12 education system, a significant increase in immigration from non-English speaking countries, and an adult education system that is now obsolete and ill-equipped to meet the 21st century needs.**
>
> — *National Commission on Adult Literacy*

My daddy lived his values through hard work. My mother raised us children, and she also was a powerful example to me. She was very patient and just always there, available, ready to help. She was one of 12 children, all of whom lived, worked and demonstrated

After a 33-year career as a teacher, Joyce Binion turned to tutoring in retirement as a way to remain engaged with her community. She says it's tough keeping adult students focused on the time required to master reading in the face of shifting priorities. Still, she stresses that reading is key to personal "independence and new opportunities."

good values and discipline. Four of her family members are ministers today.

I don't know whether we can totally overcome the problem of functional illiteracy in Alabama and the nation, but we certainly can do better. Parents can be much more interested and involved in their children's learning and education. We need them to be. We also need many more adults to become tutors for those who are outside of the educational system; they are often unemployed and struggling to survive and support families of their own.

The first student I tutored was a lady in her 40s who could read a bit but who struggled to understand and pronounce words. Her first goal was to be able to read a recipe. She said she could cook because she'd watched her mother cook, and she could cook what she'd always cooked, but she wanted to be able to read a recipe book to try to cook new things. One day she brought in a recipe for green bean casserole. She wanted to learn how to read and understand the recipe so she could make green bean casserole for Thanksgiving dinner for her family.

We sat down and went through that recipe and focused on the critical pieces of it—the amount of time to cook, the temperature, ingredients and so forth. And she went home and did it! At another session she told me she had received a traffic ticket for going the wrong way down a one-way street. Now, just think for a moment: Here's a woman in her 40s, she had a job, she had a car, she passed her driving test, but she couldn't read the words on a one-way street sign.

It's so difficult for adults to stick with a reading program as long as they need to. They all start with good intentions: They come in for lessons, we work together, and then something happens, and more often than not they simply stop coming at some point. Sometimes if they miss a few sessions, they don't want to return because they're embarrassed that they were absent. Some simply get discouraged because progress is slower than they want. For others, their lives just change and reading tumbles down the list of priorities. One lady I tutored became occupied with her children, especially one daughter who experienced some serious problems in school. Life happens every day, and for many it's difficult to stay focused on reading.

With others, you can see progress in their work. That's exciting. And you know they can see progress because it shows in their faces. Some of my best memories as a teacher are about watching second and third graders come to realize that they could read. They had learned to read, and they knew they could read. That awareness would light up their faces and warm my heart so much.

In the end, reading is about independence. That's the best message we can give: Reading increases your independence and your opportunities. Most want a better job; most want to stand on their own; most want a better life for themselves and their children. Reading's about a future, isn't it? About building that future? It's a simple but incredibly powerful idea that you can shape the future you want—if you can read.

8. Reading delivers freedom

The story of **Richard Sweeney, Sr.,** teacher, Multicultural Resource Center, Hoover

I was born in Montpelier, Vermont, and later moved to Cleveland, Ohio where I attended John Carroll University, a Jesuit college. I majored in English and minored in history and philosophy. I also earned 21 hours of Latin, which was required for the B.A. degree. I spent five years in the newspaper field. It was a great opportunity for writing, but the pay wasn't something I wanted to live with for the rest of my life.

So I went into advertising and sales promotion for Newspaper Enterprises Association, and then I took an administrative job with American Greeting Cards Corporation, followed by a position as advertising director for a small manufacturing concern. Later I went into the life insurance business, eventually becoming a member of the board of a company which was subsequently purchased by Protective Life Insurance here in Birmingham in 1978. In 1983 we moved from Cleveland to Birmingham. I retired from the company in 2000.

I've learned a few lessons over the years. One was something my dad said when I was 14 or 15 years old. I grew up in a lower middle class family where money was tight. My father said that "People with more money are not necessarily better, smarter or more talented than you are. And people with less money are not necessarily worse, dumber or less talented than you are. Be nice to the little people."

I learned another lesson at American Greetings. I fouled up one day and made a bad projection on sales.

When I went to my boss and told him I'd really messed up, his response was: "That's great. I'm glad to hear that. We've got a quota of 10 foulups a week, and you've only been coming in with one or two." The attitude was, don't be afraid to make mistakes, and that's a great environment in which to work. And later, when I was a manager, that helped me to be more tolerant.

Another lesson was about delegating responsibility. I was commanding officer of a National Guard Unit, an antiaircraft battery, and I had the idea to turn command of the unit over to one of my assistant lieutenants for a day to help him develop. So I did; I told him it was his unit that day. Then something happened, and I stepped back in. But the lieutenant looked at me and said, "Did you give me command of the unit today or not?" So the lesson was, when you delegate, let it go.

The Multicultural Resource Center in Hoover started in 2003. The city had a problem then with primarily Hispanic immigrants who were looking for day labor jobs. They would gather on the street corners in Hoover and wait for work pickups. And when a car would stop to collect several, they would all rush the vehicle to get work. This created lots of traffic and safety problems in Hoover, so the city wanted to get them off the street, and they sent out invitations for proposals to accommodate the day laborers.

> **One-third of foreign-born adults, and 44 percent of Hispanic Americans, do not have a high school diploma; 80 percent of them report not speaking English well or at all.**
>
> — *National Commission on Adult Literacy*

The Catholic Diocese of Birmingham responded with a program that was eventually accepted. The city then gave a building for the project, and it was called the Multicultural Resource Center. There was a classroom, offices, a food facility, restroom, and so forth. And there was an area where workers could gather and be picked up for work. They developed a system where there was a signup list for the workers, and they each gave a dollar each to the coordinator who handled the signup sheet because he couldn't work. Typically 60-90 workers might get jobs through that method. The center provided them coffee and donuts in the morning. Shipley's Donuts in Hoover gave most of their leftover donuts to the center.

They offered ESL classes from the beginning, and I taught a couple of those. I started teaching on a regular basis in 2005. Translation services also were available at the center for local schools, for example, for parents who didn't speak English; they would need help at parent-teacher conferences. I think they have translators available in about 15 languages.

But some of Hoover's citizens complained about the noise and activities at the center. They felt the center encouraged Hispanics to stay in Hoover, and some just wanted to get rid of them. They felt that closing down the center would eliminate the problem. So the city broke the contract they had entered with us and gave two weeks' notice to the Catholic Diocese to get out of the center.

One of the men in the Saint Peter the Apostle parish, Tom Michaels, owned an office building, and he let the center relocate there, rent free. That was in 2005, and so the center relocated to Victory Lane in Hoover, a much smaller facility. The day laborer program was discontinued because there simply wasn't room for it, and the focus shifted to social services and translation services. They recently took on a food and clothing collection facility, when Tom had more space available. The center wants to help the Hispanic community become part of the Hoover community.

I teach at the center for a minimum of two hours a week, and often more. I teach English as a second language and provide teaching help for those who primarily speak Spanish—reading, comprehension and some very basic math skills. Yesterday, for example, I wanted to get into the concept of discounts and sales. I use simple arithmetic and math examples. If it's an $80 jacket, and you get 50 percent off, then you pay $40. They understand that, and it leads into discussion of "plus" and "minus," for example, which leads to "add" and "subtract." You give them the concepts.

> **Fewer than five percent of those who could benefit from adult literacy and education programs are actually enrolled in classes. Seventy-eight percent of English as a Second Language programs in the country have waiting lists.**
>
> — *Literacy Powerline, 2010*

All the people I work with are adults, and most of them know some basic English. I take a word and use it in a sentence. Then I go over every word in the sentence for pronunciation, which is what they really want to know. They want to know the words, and they want to be able to pronounce them. Our instructor training by the Literacy Council in Birmingham highlights that the classroom belongs to the student. What they want to talk about is what you talk about, so I start the class by asking my students what words or phrases they've come across that they have questions about. One lady yesterday said, "pick on;" what does it mean to "pick on" someone? I checked in the English/Spanish dictionary, and some synonyms were "annoy" and "bother," and those concepts they could understand. But in Spanish, one of the synonyms was "molesto," which of course has a different meaning, and so we talked about that. Then I write sentences on the board with each of the terms in a sentence so they can see it. But the idea is to work with the terms closest to the students, based on their needs and interests.

One of the topics that comes up frequently is how to apply for a job. I've held classes on going to visit the doctor, and how to ask questions and understand some basic medical terms. I've held classes on how to call utility companies for service. I've also taught them how "por favor," which is "please" in English, can open doors and keep them open. I encourage the adults to use the word frequently because it will help them. We go over restaurant menus and menu items on occasion. These are some examples of practical education.

I enjoy the work. I see the great need that exists within the Hispanic community for language skills, and I believe the value in getting them to be comfortable and integrated into this country is enormous. Many years ago I read a story in the *Reader's Digest* about a woman who couldn't read. But as she began to improve her reading skills, she said she was overcome with joy in just driving down the street and being able to read the store signs. That store sold shoes. This one sold hats. That big one sold groceries, and so forth. She was exhilarated to discover the link between the words and what they represented. Until I read that story, I really didn't comprehend what people couldn't understand, or what they lacked, if they couldn't read.

I believe that education and the ability to read deliver freedom to people. They lose the dependency they have on others and gain freedom. If you read, you have the freedom to understand, negotiate and explore life. Imagine yourself in Mexico City, for example, and you can't read or understand Spanish. You're totally dependent on others for directions, meaning, travel, even safety. My philosophy in teaching is that I'm trying to give people the freedom to move about Hoover, to move around the city of Birmingham, to move about the entire country—by being able to read.

9. Education in the genes

The story of **Julia Chancy,** PLUS Volunteer Coordinator, Shelton State Community College

MY family has greatly influenced me. My mother was a librarian, and my father was a mechanical engineer. My mother made sure that we attended Sunday school and church—not just to attend, but to teach in Sunday school and volunteer in the community. At a young age we were involved with the March of Dimes, and she often took us to visit our neighbor who had polio.

My grandmother was left a widow in WWII, and her oldest son was killed overseas. My father served in the war and was unable to come home for the funeral or to help her, so she had to go to work. She had been to a secretarial school, so she worked in Montgomery in the state government offices. She came to realize how much it would have helped her if she'd had a little more education.

Both of my grandfathers were inventors. One was a pharmacist, and he invented a bug spray called "Sweet Dreams." But his biggest regret was that he didn't have enough education to know about getting a patent on the product. So it became the Gulf Company's insect spray. My other grandfather owned a casket and funeral company that was located on a busy street corner in Baltimore. He invented—I'm not even sure what you call it—a turn-around entrance, where you could pull in and curve around and exit, without having to back your vehicle onto the street.

He and another man also were among the first to own an automated bowling alley, which was located on the top story of the funeral home. Unfortunately, he lost his business to a silent partner who pretty much sold it out from under him. When my grandfather became paralyzed, he took in this silent partner to help out and keep things going. But he lost the business, and he always said that if he'd known something more about law, if he'd had more education, he could have prevented that. So he wanted my sisters and me to become lawyers.

It was my father's ambition for us three girls that we be able to support ourselves. You can start to see how important education was in my family. So we all attended the University of Alabama and chose education. My sisters were in elementary education, but I wanted to work with older children or adults because I identified more with them. I started teaching history and English in junior high school in Huntsville when my husband was in the army. Then we moved back to Tuscaloosa, and I taught in the county school system for about 28 years. After that I was with the Tuscaloosa County Board of Education, and I worked with the Adult Education and the PLUS program at Shelton State.

I've been a reading tutor and involved in adult education for about seven years. A friend who worked in adult education shared stories with me about how gratifying it was to work with adults—to see them

> **Among adults at the lowest level of literacy proficiency, 43 percent live in poverty. Among adults with strong literacy skills, only four percent live in poverty.**
>
> — *U.S. Department of Education, 1998*

progress with their jobs and lives through education. She felt that you could make a real impact, and her stories inspired me to become involved.

The most powerful and poignant experience I've had as a tutor was with a middle-aged gentleman who told me he couldn't read because he had brain damage as a result of his father beating him severely when he was a child—because he couldn't read! He did have some brain injury, and progress with him was very slow. But he was always cheerful, and he always showed up. He never missed. We made progress with life skills, though he didn't move past the third-grade reading level. But he learned to read his bus schedule, for example. He could read part of his Sunday school message and lesson. We looked at job applications and worked through those. We read the TV guide out of the newspaper. He also learned to read and understand his lease. I tried to help him understand the concept of interest charges and interest rates when you charge items, but that was difficult for him.

We worked together about two years. He believed he was making progress, and he was enormously proud of that. He regretted not being able to return to elementary school to study, but of course he was too old for that. The saddest thing I saw was how some people took advantage of him. He bought a ring for a lady, and he had signed one of those payment forms that you can hardly ever pay off because the interest rates are so high. Someone made a great deal of money due to his inability to read. And the lady he married— she took all of his money and then left him. His inability to read led him into being a victim of others, and I just felt so sad about that.

Another one of my students was an older lady, now in her 70s, who was functionally illiterate and reading at the third-grade level when she began our program. She's progressed now to a sixth-grade reading level and could enter an adult education program if she wanted to. But she likes one-on-one tutoring, and she's so embarrassed about her reading skills that she still doesn't want anyone to know that she is getting help with her reading.

She's a board member for a community organization, and she didn't want them to know how little she could read. But now she says she can join in conversations. She can read notes at the board meeting. She has a library card and checks out books from her library. She had a granddaughter who came to live with her, and she tutored her to improve her reading. She's more active with her Sunday school and participates much more. Her tutor helped her register so that she voted for the first time in her life in 2008, and that was exciting for her. Today, she's still working with a tutor, one-on-one, and she still doesn't want anyone to know about it!

For many people, learning to read is the least of their worries; they just don't have time to spend on reading. They have family issues, they are looking for work, they are raising children, and so forth. Of course, unemployment is the big issue right now. So many people who had construction or manual labor jobs lost them, and work is so hard to find. Employers are able to pick and choose, and they're going to select someone who can read and follow directions and write things, if needed. For some others who work in mines, or towing companies, or manufacturing plants, their jobs now require them to be able to read a safety

A life-long educator, Julia Chancy believes the literacy movement needs to recruit a new front-line of volunteers who can spot people who can't read and then refer them to programs to get the help they need.

manual and pass a safety test, and they can't do that without reading.

Illiteracy is a big problem just among those individuals who are visible, who've asked for help or joined adult education programs. But there are so many others around us that we don't see unless we look closely for them. For example, almost every time I go to Wal-Mart and stand in the checkout line, I see an individual who can't write out a check. They ask the cashier to do it for them. Or, they get help and directions from the sales clerk when they ask, "If I get two of these, what does it say on here about how much that would cost?" Or they might ask the clerk, "How am I supposed to use this product?"

You can observe signs in other places, too. I've noticed what a problem it is in the doctor's office when the nurse says, here's your prescription, and here are the directions for taking this medicine. Sometimes the nurse will have time when the patient says I don't understand this, or I can't read that, but often they don't have the time, or won't take the time to help that person understand. And I've seen many patients, when the nurse gives them the medicine and tells them what to do, they just have this blank look. They can't read the label, and they may not know what to do, but it seems clear they can't read the medication label.

So I believe that beyond the ongoing tutoring programs in our communities and the tutors in our schools, we also need volunteers in medical facilities, in employment offices, and elsewhere. They are needed to help people who can't understand what they're reading. They could be a kind of front-line network that recognizes those who can't read and provides assistance on location, and then serves as a referral agency. That would take the literacy fight out into the community and make it more visible.

One of the most difficult things is to get people who need help to take the steps to receive that help. I

> Among the 30 member countries of the Organization for Economic Cooperation and Development (OECD), the U.S. ranks 11th in the percentage of adults with a high school diploma and is the only country where younger adults are less educated than the previous generation.
>
> — *National Commission on Adult Literacy*

get referrals for people who say they want to learn to read. I make an appointment with them, but then they don't show up. So I call them back and make another appointment, and still they don't show up. I feel like once they come in and get started, they will stay and learn. But they have to take some big steps to make that happen. First, they have to let someone know they need help, and that's a huge step. Then they actually have to make the effort to meet in person with us, which is another big step. And then they have to commit to a regular schedule of reading sessions and show up for them. Unfortunately, we lose people at every step in that process.

Adults drop out of reading programs due to difficulties with program content, slow progress, feelings of inferiority and family responsibilities and work-related obligations.

— J.D. Fliss, Introduction to Adult Literacy— Portfolio

When someone calls, I try to be encouraging. I don't want to frighten them, or make it overly difficult. I tell them we'll have a conversation and find out where they need to begin reading, and then we'll start right there. I just try to reassure them that they are past the scary part, they made the phone call. I tell them that making the call is the bravest thing they can do, and the rest of this is not going to be difficult. The tough part is over.

Once they come into the office, I tell them I'm going to find a caring person for their tutor, someone who will keep all of this confidential, which is the one thing they all want. That person will meet with them twice a week and help them with their reading. Their first question is usually, how long is this going to take? I tell them I will get a tutor to stay with them for as long as it takes for them to feel comfortable with their reading. The people who need something related to their jobs immediately are the ones who are most frustrated because learning to read takes longer than anyone wants it to. But I always tell them it will take forever if they don't start.

10. Closing the deficit

The story of **Shirley Bingham,** adult tutor and schoolteacher, Bessemer

I grew up in a single parent home. My mother was very independent; she raised me without help from anyone, with no child support available. She was smart and advanced in her job. She worked at Maxwell AFB and then at a veteran's hospital. She kept moving up in the system, and when she went as high as she could in Montgomery, the only way she could advance further in her career was to move to Birmingham, which she did. She worked for the Social Security Administration in Birmingham.

I like to say I am educated far beyond my intelligence. I have a B.S. in education from the University of Alabama in Tuscaloosa, with concentrations in English and Spanish. I also have an M.A. from the university in Birmingham and an educational specialist degree and an ESL Certification, also from Birmingham. I've always taught English and Spanish, all the grade levels from kindergarten to adults. And I've had some wonderful international education, too.

I lived in Guatemala for two years, where I worked for the Foreign Mission Board. That gives one a unique perspective on your own country. When I was in high school I was able to spend six weeks in Mexico with a group of students at the University of Monterey. I did my student teaching for the University in Barranquilla, Colombia, in South America. I always liked Spanish in school, so I had planned for a while to teach Spanish and English in school. The further I went, the more I enjoyed the Spanish.

My husband, Ben, and I also have traveled abroad on summer mission trips. We spent six weeks in the high jungle of Bolivia. We've been in Guatemala twice. They are always dual-purpose trips: There's a construction project, something we leave behind that is helpful to a community or group, and there's some evangelistic outreach. Usually we do outreach to children through the use of puppets. In South America people love to go to the parks with their families and town squares on Sundays. So we find a place in a park, we set up a little puppet stage, have some music and then when people gather around we always have a native Spanish speaker talk. We distribute literature and then contact anyone in the area who might want to respond to our appeal.

In Alabama, 40 percent of children entering fourth grade are unable to read at grade level.

— *Tuscaloosa Chamber of Commerce*

Certain values are very important to me, and my husband and I hope to pass them on to our grandchildren. Responsibility is one of those values. We see parents today who don't want to accept responsibility for their children's actions. Some parents want to blame others, keep their child from accepting responsibility for their own actions. How does that help children? Values of right and wrong are important. And independence— not depending on the government for everything. I'd say our family values are just pretty much traditional Christian values. My guess is that probably a lot of the tutors in programs like this one have a very similar outlook—the desire to help and make the world a better place.

Family is crucial. My parents were divorced, and I am old enough that it was uncommon at the time. I felt different, like I was left out. I feel that if I had had a more complete, loving family that I might have had more self-confidence in school. But the primary experience that shaped who I am is becoming a Christian. This happened when I was very young, so it was a big help to me all the way through school and life. My mother always took me to church, even if she didn't always go. And my Sunday school teacher played a big role. She talked about how we have a Father in Heaven who loves us, and not having an earthly father, I really paid attention to that. I don't think it meant as much to the other children, but it did to me.

My aunt Erline also was important to me. She was never married and she was an educator all of her life. First, she was a teacher, then a principal and administrator for years, and then she went to the State Department. She was a mentor to me, and I wanted to follow a similar path, but leaving out the principal part! She helped other people all of her life—students and people in her family. She was influential in her community; people knew, treasured and respected her.

I always thought it would be the neatest, coolest gift to be able to give an adult the gift of reading. Isn't that a great thing? So, then Cleon Rogers showed up at our church one Sunday. He's a medical student who grew up in Germany, and who involved medical students in a local organization called M-POWER. He got the students to go down to the free medical clinic they have and donate blankets, supplies and their time to serve at this clinic. Cleon mentioned at church that

Shirley Bingham points out that technology, including video games, can be a deterrent to students learning to read. As a tutor, she helps manage their expectations and tries to serve as a strong role model—something often lacking in their lives.

there was need for volunteers to do administrative paperwork at the clinic, so several of us volunteered. And then along came the opportunity to participate in a literacy program in Bessemer. Five of us went through the tutor training, and that's how we wound up here.

Charnessa is my first student. All I can say about Charnessa is that I am blessed because she is so faithful. She does her homework. She does her reading. She does her little projects that I give her. She is just great. She's not a beginner. She's already reading at about a second-grade level.

Now, Charnessa is very smart, and she's a good guesser. And what she's learned how to do is read the first part of the word, which she does well, and then guess at the last part.

So I have been working on getting her to focus on the last part of the word. Because I'm a teacher, I have teaching materials, little flip books and things that we can use to focus on the last parts or syllables of words. She can do these, and they help her remember the endings. She also knows long and short sounds. I also made lists of words that are close but different, for example, like "fat" and "fate" or "hat" and "hate." We also started on improving her reading vocabulary. She has great memory when we read stories.

One day, Dave Holt dropped by. He's not usually here. But he stopped by to say hello, and in the course of a brief conversation, Charnessa and I brought him up to date on what we were reading. At a certain point, Charnessa asked, "Do you want me to read it?" And she read it for him and did a great job. He started bragging on her, complimenting her, and she was so proud. That was an opportunity for her to shine, and it was a nice moment for all of us.

> **In 2009, only about one-third of U.S. fourth graders read at a "proficient level" or better, up only slightly from 1992.**
>
> — *Greg Tippo.*
> *USA Today*

Adult learners have so many complications to deal with on their road to learning. They have schedule issues, work conflicts, family complications, finding the time that it takes. You have to have the time to practice, too, whatever the skill is. Motivation is another problem because progress is very slow. Reading is not an overnight achievement. We know that if a student doesn't learn to read by the third or fourth grade, it's an uphill battle after that. Another issue is child care. Is it available and affordable?

We deal with many issues for school-age students, too—lack of reading materials at home, lack of adult modeling, not having adults read with them from an early age on. Another big issue is television, gaming devices, X-Box. Those things hurt reading because they take the place of books and lessen the need for imagination. I know they say there are some advantages with TV, but I've read that TV images change about every three seconds on screen, and that's going to affect concentration and focus. When you go from that to reading, it's difficult because reading requires sharp focus and concentration.

Another problem is not having boundaries in the home, discipline. Children don't have to sit down and be quiet. If they want to run around and make noise, they are allowed to. They may self-stimulate a great deal. We see so many kinds of problems like this in the school where I teach. Children from problem homes also don't usually have rich background experiences, or knowledge. By a problem home I mean one where you probably have a single parent who may be a drug user, drug dealer, alcohol abuser. We have students in our school who don't know where they are going to be on any given night, or where they are going to sleep. And you have teenage parents, too. Others are dependent on the government for assistance, and so there are often not clearly defined work goals. They have no sense of reaching and achieving for something.

Many of these issues go back to families, homes and early childhood. Any attempt to make up that deficit is difficult. I think that one adult helping one child to learn to read, one-on-one tutoring, is the best hope we have. It would almost take one adult per child, or one adult tutor for each adult learner, to try to make up that deficit in learning and background knowledge.

The schools try to make up some of the deficit by taking kids to the zoo, to the theater. That's really important for our kids because many of them have never been either place. My students, and I teach Hispanic students, didn't know what the Olympics were, or what the word meant. Nothing. So I got on the Internet and gathered them around my computer, and we looked at a number of clips and talked about the Olympics. The idea was, when they hear the word again, they will have some background and a mental image of what the word is and means. This also provided a good opportunity for some vocabulary study. It's almost like adopting a child to help them, to try to make up for what their family has not given them, if they have an immediate family at all.

I mentioned role models earlier. The role models for many young people today are sports figures and rock stars who are not always good role models. Sometimes they are tattoo-covered, body-pierced, multiple partners of the same or opposite sex, who promote partying—not education. I asked my principal recently whether we had any graduates of this school who went on to be successful. She said many had. So I asked if we had any young enough that could come to school and serve as a role model—someone the kids could see and talk to and be inspired a little bit beyond what they see in their small everyday world. We can't change the role models, or whom kids idolize, but we can try to bring them in contact with good role models, too.

Stories of Obligation

Passing it on

11. Sweet potato pie

The story of **Charnessa Moore,** adult learner, Bessemer

I was born to Laverne and Abby Wilson, and I don't know what happened to them, but my grandmother raised me, and she did a wonderful job. My sisters and brothers, we all stayed with grandma. She was the center of our lives. She dressed us up and took us to church every Sunday morning. She had us up at six o'clock. She'd bathe us and wash and straighten our hair every week before church. We had to be clean and just so for her. Only one way to go to church, according to her, and that was *her* way.

She was very strict. When it came on 4:30 in the afternoon, she'd make us come in off the street, come up on the porch. When the porch light came on, we had to be up on that porch. She wanted us safe. She taught me how to cook, and I still love to cook today. I love to do steamed cabbages and baked pork chops, collard greens and beef roasts. My favorite meal is baked chicken and brown rice, and especially sweet potato pie. That's the best. Grandma was a strong, proud, tough lady who was a real role model for me and my sisters and brothers.

Some of her rubbed off on me, I guess. I have three little ladies that go to my church, and I like to spend time with them—washing, straightening and curling their hair. I also have a little lady I sit with three days a week; I go in and bathe her and take care of her for the nursing staff.

I was in special education throughout school. I did a co-op program and was a cook in the cafeteria when I was in the 11th and 12th grades. I did this while I was pregnant, and I had my first baby when I was in the 12th grade. After I graduated, I went back and worked as a cook in the school for about 10 years. Then I slipped and fell on a wet floor and injured my knee so I couldn't work anymore.

Now I'm 33 years old, and I have a husband and two kids. Jeremy, my 14-year-old son, plays football, basketball and wrestles, and now he's in the jazz band. I have a 4-year-old who's in daycare—Little Ted, or Ted the third—and he's real excited about going to school just like his big brother. My husband works at Vulcan Materials. He taught me how to drive. He supports me and the kids, and he always supports me in what I try to do—gives me some confidence. I was in a reading program before, from about 1999-2002. We worked on three books, and I received some certificates for that time. Then I had another baby, and only some months ago I called the library and asked if they had any reading programs. They put me in touch with Mr. Dave Holt, and I started in November with Miss Shirley, my tutor.

Every year, one in three adults—more than 1.2 million people—drops out of U.S. high schools.

— *National Commission on Adult Literacy*

I want to be able to read *to* my baby now, and to read *with* him later. I buy little storybooks that I can read to him, but I want to go a lot higher. I want to read to him when he gets older, too, not just as a little kindergartener. Every night I try to spend at least 15 minutes and read a little story to my son after he gets his bath. I sit on the side of the bed and read. I pick a book that I know he likes and one that I know I can read good.

I also want to be able to read better for myself. Right now I can read little books like *The Cat in the Hat* and *Mr. Colorful*. I also can read some of the little comics in the Sunday newspaper. But I want to be able to read more; I want to be able to read the Bible. Me and Miss Shirley, we always read a Bible story before we start class. And when I'm in church now I can follow what the preacher reads from the Bible. I like that because I used to have a hard time trying to do that, but now I can follow along. I spend about an hour a day, maybe more, on my reading.

We meet every Tuesday and Wednesday for the reading program. I do my homework at night, and I have Bible studies I have to read, little scriptures. When I come to class the next day, I have to tell Miss Shirley what I read. The hardest thing for me now is some of the words—they get longer and harder, just like the stories. It takes a long time. But Miss Shirley is sweet, she's nice and I can depend on her.

Reading helps me in my daily life, too. When I first started, I didn't have a driver's license because my husband had to read everything to me about driving. So I kept going, and it took me 10 times before I passed the driving test, but I made it. I can also now read little signs along the road. I couldn't do that before, and that's nice. I'm not quite so blind now. I'm starting to read the world.

And I can read recipes now. When my grandmother died, my brothers and sisters and I divided up all the recipes in her book. I liked the ones with the sweet potato pies, and things like that. Now that I can read, I'm thinking about starting my own recipe book.

I know other people need reading help, too. I'd encourage them to pray first, and then go out to their library and see if some reading programs are available. If they want me to go with them, I'd show them the way. I'd tell them that reading's enjoyable. It's fun to read. And you need to be able to read for your children and grandchildren.

12. How you treat people

The story of **Stephen Hannum,** provider services manager, the Literacy Council in Birmingham

I come from a family where my brothers are either Ph.D.s or CPAs, my parents are well educated, and my grandfather was the dean of the engineering school at Auburn. There were always books around the house, and we didn't even discuss not being able to read. I just assumed everyone was like me with lots of books, education and opportunities. I didn't learn much about illiteracy until I was working as a tennis professional in Atlanta. I was in my early 20s then, not married, and I went with a couple of my friends to volunteer for the literacy program. We did it because we wanted to meet young ladies, not really for altruistic purposes.

But I was assigned a student almost immediately. He was about my age, a construction worker, and he'd arrive at our sessions late afternoon or early evening, dirty clothes, all worn out from a hard day on the job. I would come in, and I wasn't rich, but money was not a concern, and there he was: fighting it all day for a chance at something that I simply took for granted—the ability to read.

He was eager to learn, and I got hooked right there. I realized that something's not fair about this. Why was I given all of this stuff and never had to work for it, and he has to work really hard during a long, physical day, and then come in and do more work? If I wanted to go buy a new car, I'd just go buy one. He couldn't do that. If I wanted to go out to eat or buy some new clothes, I could just do it. But he couldn't. He didn't have any of those possibilities, and it just didn't seem fair to me.

When a job opportunity came along in Tuscaloosa, I moved there and worked as a tennis pro and a coach at Alabama. There wasn't an adult literacy program in Tuscaloosa then, so I volunteered as a tutor through the County Board of Education. I was assigned to work with a woman in her late 20s, a mother of a couple of kids, who never learned to read. There was no place to go for the tutoring session, so we would sit outside and work on the side steps of the education building right along Greensboro Avenue when the weather was nice.

Her story was the same as the construction worker: She came from a family that didn't have the advantages I did. So I tutored for a while, and I continued to have a decent career in tennis, but I got tired of it. I came to the clear realization that too often my biggest decisions in any given day were whether to return to the swimming pool, or to get another shrimp salad. I knew that I had to do more than that in life, so I changed professions and began work in the nonprofit world.

> **The cost to our economy [of illiteracy] ... is very great. The cost to our presumptions and our credibility as a democracy is greater still. The cost in needless human pain may be the greatest price of all.**
>
> — *Jonathan Kozol*
> *Illiterate America*

After more education and some work with the boys and Girls Clubs in Tuscaloosa, I landed here at The Literacy Council in Birmingham, where I've been for about five years. I work with different agencies that

As Birmingham's area coordinator of literacy programs, Steve Hannum believes that the cost of resolving illiteracy in America would be more than offset by the savings realized across society.

provide literacy services in the area. Some are well-funded, they've been around for years and they know what they are doing. Some are just getting started and need direction. My role is to assist any of those agencies in their development and activities in any way possible. There's not much here that's routine. I like that. I can interact with Ph.D.s who have worked in education and literacy for many years, and then the next phone call might be from a 19-year-old who dropped out of school in 8th grade, barely knows the alphabet and is looking for some help or direction.

Many of the important lessons I've learned in life go back to my parents. Frequently, if I'm in some situation and having to make a decision, I often stop and think, now what would daddy have told me? Probably the most important lesson I learned from them is this: *All that really matters is how you treat other people.* This seems to be a theme in all the major religions, too, so when I'm in a position to make a decision, all I really have to do is follow this guideline, this golden rule. If you keep it in the back of your mind and be guided by it, you're going to be just fine in your decision making. I think the answers are almost always in our hearts, not our heads.

We run into some typical and recurring barriers to adult literacy. Some of them relate to family matters—I can't find a babysitter, or the car won't start, or my wife had to use the car to get to work so I can't make it in for our session today. Some are employment barriers—my shift at work got changed so I can't come in for tutoring anymore, or I found a part-time job that prevents me from coming to tutoring. Personal issues are another issue. They cover a wide range: a lack of belief in the possibility of success because I've failed so many times, or nobody else in my family can read so why should I, or I've gotten this far without learning how to read, so why learn now?

Institutional barriers refer to things that service providers—community colleges, libraries and churches—do or don't do well. For example, do they provide convenient schedules for learners? Do they help with transportation or childcare? Do they warmly welcome adult learners, or do they initially overwhelm them with forms and tests to complete? Their response to such barriers is often to think, I can't do this, and so they drop out. Or maybe they are in dire financial straits, or they are on probation, or they are drug or alcohol abusers. There are so many reasons why they might fail and why they even expect to fail.

So here's the key thing: Part of that adult learner's success is directly dependent upon the literacy instructor or tutor, or the teacher's ability to help that person resolve any of these issues and others, too. These are the kinds of things that someone in social work would be more apt to do, but they fall to the reading tutor in the literacy arena. Some really experienced and seasoned tutors told me, "Hey, you don't really need to know about vowels and consonants. What you need to know is how to help someone resolve family problems, personal problems, credit issues and things like that."

To keep people coming back, it's sometimes as simple as making sure that they have some success in every meeting. They need to feel like they are making progress. And it's also important to keep the reading relevant to their interests and goals—something they can see that adds meaning and is useful to their life. If that person came to tutoring to learn to read the Bible for church, for example, then you need to get them to the Bible as quickly as you can.

> **The relationship of literacy and poverty is undeniable. Children in professional families hear an average of 2,153 words per hour, an average of 1,251 words per hour in working class families, and only 616 words per hour in welfare families.**
>
> — *B. Hart & T.R. Risley, Meaningful Differences in the Everyday Experience of Young American Children, 1995*

We can solve the literacy problem. It's not free, but if you look at the cost of fixing the literacy problem versus the costs of fixing some other major social problems, there's no comparison. We don't have to build prisons. We don't have to build hospitals or purchase expensive equipment to solve the problem. You can teach someone how to read with a newspaper. So many of society's problems don't have clear answers, but literacy does. I think the solution is relatively simple and inexpensive. And we are all part of it. We all have to be part of it.

Now some people see those numbers about illiteracy and they say that's not my problem. I don't have to worry about it. My kids are educated, so am I and we have money. But if you find somebody who says this, then ask them this: When you take your car to the shop to have it worked on, what if the guy who's fixing the brakes can't read? Maybe they say, I don't have to worry about it because I go to a car dealer who has a trained staff. My response to that is: What if the guy in the lane next to you is driving 75 miles an hour, and he fixed his own brakes, and he couldn't read the installation instructions? Is it your problem then? The thing is, the literacy problem affects all of us.

The prisons are full of people who can't read. If a person is homeless and can't read, they are likely to always be homeless. Or if they are an abused spouse who can't read, then they are likely to always be abused because they can't be independent without reading skills. The list of

> **A country that was founded on the principles of free speech, free press, and the freedom of religion—all rights tied inextricably to words—is fast becoming an illiterate nation. The ability to read is the foundation for everyday life. Indeed, virtually none of the major issues we face as a nation today can be successfully overcome until we eradicate illiteracy.**
>
> — *Wish You Well Foundation, 2010*

scenarios just goes on and on. If you can't read and don't improve your ability to read, you are likely to be firmly stuck in your situation, whatever it is. And your kids may be stuck, too.

This makes literacy a foundational issue, so it is not just that other guy's problem or their problem, it's yours, too. It is our problem. Whether you look at it from a golden rule perspective, or a purely business perspective, or even a public safety perspective in the sense of the person driving next to you on the freeway, it's everyone's problem. It touches everybody.

13. Pass the gift to your child

The story of **LaTonya Scates,** adult learner, Bessemer

I come to the library often to get books for my little girl. She's in kindergarten and just starting to read. I can read, but I read slower than other people. I have always been shy about my reading. When I was little I had asthma real bad and missed a lot of school. I always seemed to be behind everyone else. The other kids could read faster than me, and they seemed to know the words better than I did. I stumbled over words a lot, so I always felt I couldn't read as well as others. But I've found out that I can read, and I've also learned that some other people who are smart people also read slowly. My problem isn't as big a problem as I thought; I just lack confidence in myself.

I've been coming in for help for a couple of months, and it started when I came in to pick up a few books one day, and I saw the notice about the literacy program. I decided there ain't nothing wrong with learning things that can help my daughter. I decided I wanted to be in the program to help my daughter— help her break down and sound out words so that she becomes a good reader, better than me.

I was born in Birmingham, and my parents live in Bessemer. They've been married about 40 years, and I lived there until I got married. My father used to work in a coal plant until he hurt his back. My mom's been a homemaker all her life. I have four sisters and two brothers. They all live in Alabama, and we spend a lot of time together. We meet at our parents' house and we cook and eat together a lot. We sit over and just enjoy our family. Family is strength for me.

I like to spend a lot of time with my little girl, who's six. We go shopping, we go to Chucky Cheese, we go to the movies. We've seen *Hotel for Dogs* and the *Princess and the Frog* and *Planet 51*. We see some of these at the dollar movie. We might stop and get some pizza, or eat popcorn or get a kid's meal there. We try to get out and do something every weekend. Another thing we do, I have some of the kids from her daycare group over, and I set up the front room like it's a camp. I have a fireplace in my apartment, and I get the sleeping bags and put them out, and we have a sleep-over for some kids in my front room in front of the fireplace. I get them different little movies to watch, and they play games and tell each other spooky stories.

> **On average, the cost to society to support each high school dropout is $127,000. A student drops out of high school every 26 seconds.**
>
> — *Literacy Powerline, 2009*

I try to read to my little girl every night. I read the books ahead of time to make sure I know the words, and if I don't then I break them down to understand and say them. I want to know the words when I read the books to her. She likes two books a lot: *Stop Picking on Me* and *The Ugly Duckling*.

I got married when I was younger because I wanted to do right by God. I didn't want to have a child out of wedlock. I stayed at home with my baby and didn't work outside the home. So I depended on him, but we ended up getting a divorce. I wish we had stayed together, but being on my own taught me a lot. So once I got divorced, I learned how to stand on my own two feet, like paying bills and discovering what life was like. So something that was bad actually turned into something quite good. I've learned a lot and earned some things on my own. I bought a car, a 2005 Grand Am Pontiac, and I lease my own apartment, and I get up and go to work—I drive a school bus—and do the things I'm supposed to do.

My parents have great influence on me. Some people look at stars or athletes as influencers, but my parents are my stars. My father is a minister, and my mother is saved, and I've never seen them smoke or drink or do anything bad. They have been great examples to me. I know when I used to come home from school, my momma always had the house cleaned, clothes pressed, always a meal on the table.

I saw my daddy always work hard. He told us that you have to do something with your life. You have to learn to depend on yourself, not on men. If you get a husband, he may not stay, so you have to learn to take care of yourself. He taught us about cars, how to change a tire or change the oil. He always said, "Nothing comes to a sleeper but a dream." Hard work, that's the greatest lesson I've learned from him. My parents have always been good role models for me. When I see them going through something, it teaches me. So why would I have to look on TV to find a role model when my parents are right there in front of me?

My little girl keeps me on the straight and narrow path, too. And I want to be a good role model for her. I don't drink or curse or go to the club; I don't want her doing things like that. I watch what I do in front of her because she watches me, all the time. If I tell her to put her seat belt on, and I've forgotten to put my seat belt on, she'll say, "Momma, you don't have your seat belt on either."

Miss Tiffany is my tutor now. She got me reading book three, and I read quite a bit of that in the first few days. I guess we did about 10 lessons the first day. I like these books; I think it's a great investment of my time. The book tells you what makes the sounds. My daughter likes the book. When she first saw it she got excited because she thought it was for her.

I really enjoy coming here. It's something I look forward to every Thursday. I feel like if something is free, and it can help you and benefit you, why not do it? I was reading a magazine one time while I was waiting for jury duty, and the article said that if you think education is expensive, try paying the cost for being ignorant! That's really expensive because you can't read things, you can't understand things. I'd rather come here and improve my reading because I want to get up to college-level reading.

What I've learned so far has helped me to be a better reader. I've learned it's okay to go a little slower. Before, I felt like something was wrong with me because I read so slowly. Miss Tiffany told me that she reads slower, too, and that's okay to make sure you understand. So, I've increased my confidence a lot, and now I can understand what letters make certain sounds. I always go downstairs and buy a couple of books in the bookstore to take home to read with my baby. Sometimes, if I'm not sure about some of the words in the book, I come back to my tutor and ask if I can read it to her first.

People also need to know how to read to protect themselves; people can scam you every day. You have to be able to read contracts and things you sign. If you can get some help for free, some one-on-one help, why not accept it?

And if you have kids, you need to be able to help them read and do their homework. So it's really good to read to your child. You can pass that gift on to your child. If they can read, your child might become the next person to cure cancer, or something great like that. Why can't you help them? If people are willing to take time to help you, why not? You can't find too many people who are willing to take time to help you.

14. *Not* getting help is the problem

The story of **Tiffany Beavers,** adult tutor, Bessemer

MY grandmother was the biggest influence on almost everything in my life. She was born in Lynette, Alabama and in her early 20s she moved to New York. She didn't know anyone there, but she made it on her own. She was independent, confident and committed to success. She became a seamstress and eventually owned her own business in that field. Then she became a beautician, and again started her own business. She never went to college, but she was the smartest person I've ever known.

She constantly encouraged me to read and get more education. I remember when I was seven or eight years old that I would sometimes say to her that I didn't have anything to do, I was bored. She would hand me a dictionary and say, "Here, read these words. You just might learn something." And I did. She wanted me to take piano lessons. And I did. I think she wanted me to be well rounded, not get bogged down and locked into my four-block radius in the neighborhood. She wanted me to know that there was this great big world beyond what I saw every day in my little neighborhood. She was a wonderful role model for me. She helped me to dream.

Thanks to my grandmother, I've always been interested in reading and language. I was born in Bayside, New York and grew up in Akron, Ohio. My high school English teacher—Mrs. Nine, just like the number— really moved me toward English language and literature, too. She had this incredible ability to make litera-

Recruited as a tutor by Dave Holt, Tiffany Beavers has been a strong advocate in Bessemer and believes that schools bear some of the responsibility for illiteracy by not confirming that students can actually read before advancing them through the system.

ture interesting. It wasn't just academic with her, it was life: She made it accessible, we understood it and we *liked* it. I remember that we read *"Beowul"f* in the 10th grade. The 10th grade! That was the first book we read in her class, and we all groaned and grumbled about it. I mean, what is a Beowulf? Why are we reading this old book? But we read it and somehow she got us so excited about the book that we couldn't wait to read more of it and talk about it. She loved what she did. She loved teaching, and she had so much passion for it that you could see it. I also truly believe that she loved each and every one of her students.

After high school I attended Wittenberg University in Springfield, Ohio, for two years and was an English major. Then I decided to take a break. It was a longer break than I planned, and I worked, got married and had two children. I worked at a bank for about five years and then at an insurance company here in Alabama. Now I'm back in school, and I'm now taking classes online at the University of Maryland. I'm not sure whether I'll pick up with my English studies, or major in communications or journalism.

During those years I read and wrote a great deal—short stories and poems. At one point I started to write a book, but I never finished it. Maybe I'll do that some day. I also like the outdoors and enjoy gardening—flower gardens. I'm leery of planting vegetables; I think the rabbits would get them. And I like travel. California is the most interesting place I've been. When I was a child, I travelled there every year by myself. My father lived in Los Angeles, and we lived in Ohio. From the time I was 6 until I was 11, I went to California every summer. That was like my big adventure as a child.

> **A nation's wealth is of at least two kinds. The kind enumerated by the GNP is dollars. The kind that cannot be enumerated by the GNP is dignity and decency and the informed and critical intelligence of human beings.**
>
> — *Jonathan Kozol,*
> *Illiterate America*

My involvement in the literacy program here was accidental. I'm a trustee at the Bessemer Library, and one day about six months ago I met Dave Holt at the circulation desk. We struck up a conversation, and he asked me if I knew of anyone who might tutor, or if I wanted to become a reading tutor. He said he could sure use more tutors. So I volunteered on the spot, and that's how I became a tutor.

LaTonya is my student now, and she inspires me. We're nearly the same age. Sometimes I wonder about what happened in our lives that was so different that I ended up tutoring her, and she didn't end up tutoring me, you know? What happened so it came out that way? She's a wonderful person. She can read, but she wants to be tutored so she can do a better job of helping her daughter read and learn. I think that's an awesome reason for learning to read. She wants to be here; no one is forcing her to. I've had other students who don't show up for appointments; they don't even call. But LaTonya wants to be here. I find it inspiring that she feels like, okay, I'm at this certain age now, but I'm not about to let it stop me from learning what I need to learn, or learning something that I can use to help my child in some way.

I know there are many in our community who need reading help, and I think communities and schools and individuals all need to work on this problem. Communities can help by removing the negative stigma associated with illiteracy. They can promote the idea far better that programs like this are available. Many people out there need help, but they just don't know they can find it at the library. They know you can get a book at the library, but I don't think people know there's a free literacy program here. So we need to do a better job to promote this program in our community.

I think the schools also need to do a better job. I don't mean do a better job of testing students in their reading. I mean making sure they can actually *read* when they cross the stage to receive their diploma— not just give them a piece of paper and push them out the door to get rid of them. Schools need to do a better job of making sure that students can read adequately, rather than just saying they can pass a standardized test. I mean, do standardized tests really do it? Is that what education is? There are so many people graduating from school who can't read adequately, but they apparently are completing the standardized tests. Like, what's wrong with that picture?

And I hope that the people who need reading help will understand that the problem is *not* that they can't read; the problem is in not getting the help they need when it's available. That's the problem and the real tragedy. If you're going to be embarrassed, be embarrassed because you didn't take advantage of the help— not that you can't read. There's help available if you can't read, and there's no shame except in not accepting that help.

Stories of Opportunity
Getting ahead

15. A genius on lawnmowers

The story of **David Sparks,** adult learner, Tuscaloosa

I grew up in Panola, Alabama, and moved to Tuscaloosa when I was 21. First job I got I worked in a bicycle shop. Then I worked on roads, steam cleaning for Kmart and other places. Then I started working on my own—cutting grass, lawns, like that. Now I drive a delivery truck for Alabama Power and deliver appliances to people. I've done the job going on five years. It's a pretty good job. The work's okay, but the pay's not so good. I want a better paying job.

The main thing is, I want to read better so I can open my own business. I want to get a better job, put back some money, have my own business. I'm one of the top men on lawnmowers. I'm a genius on lawnmowers. You got problems with a mower, I can fix them. I do riding mowers, push mowers. Any lawnmower ever been to my house, it left running. One guy brought a lawnmower to my house, parts all over the back of the truck. Two days later, he picked it up, running fine. If I had my own business, I'd be working on lawnmowers, weed eaters, blowers, power equipment, like that. People always have to do some grass cutting, so I think it'd be a good business.

> **Literacy can be thought of as a currency in this society.**
>
> — *U.S. Department of Education, 1993*

I came into the reading program about four months ago. I saw the ad on TV about that Literacy Edge group, and Miss Chancy at Shelton State got me lined

David Sparks is motivated to read in order to establish his own lawnmower business. He considers fixing mowers a personal passion. His lessons have already helped him master the GPS for his current job of delivering appliances. "Reading can get you from point A to point B, and maybe a lot of other places after B," he says.

up with a tutor. I like him a lot. He works me hard, but that's good. I want to better myself, and he the one can help me do it. He breaks reading down, like cutting a pie, piece by piece. I got into the first book, and I read that real easy. I'm in the second book now.

He taught me some things that in all my years I didn't know, like how to read sentences, and how they work in paragraphs. He taught me what quotation marks are, and periods, commas, like that. And he's teaching me numbers, how to pronounce them. I read stories to him. I meet him at the library every Tuesday and Thursday night, one hour each night.

I like to stay busy, not just sit around. Give me something to do. I'm a van man at the church. I pick up people on Sundays and take them to church. I'm always helping out at church, cut grass, whatever they might need.

I'm good with kids, too. Summer time, their bike breaks down, I fix it. They need a patch, I patch the tire. Their lawnmower breaks down, I put a spark plug in, or a pull rope, like that. I try to help kids because a lot of kids now got single parents. If one of them need to make a few dollars, I sometimes pick one up for a job, give them some work. You got to learn work and how to do things at a young age. If you teach kids some skills, help them out when they young, they'll remember you when they older. They'll appreciate what you done.

Fifty-five percent of Alabama's adults function at literacy levels inadequate to meet the demands of a modern technical society.

— *Alabama State Workforce Development Council*

Sometimes I take kids fishing. I love to fish—bream, bass, catfish. Sometimes I go down to Fosters. Buddy got a private catfish pond there. Another buddy, halfway to Gordo, he got a lake. We fish there. I work on his lawn mowers, and then we go fishing.

My mother died when I was three, so my grandmother was a big influence in my life. She taught me how to cook, sew, iron. I was cooking four meals a day when I was 12 years old. I cooked for everybody in the family. Now I'm married, I cook meals for my wife. Whatever you want: meat loaf, collard greens, cornbread, fish. I like to cook, but I don't like it better than I do working on lawnmowers. That's my hobby.

Reading helps me in my work because I have to open up the appliance box to get the name, who's it going to, like that. I can read the names now and take that information and put it in the GPS to get to the right address. I couldn't do that before. I'm learning to do more writing, too. But the best part now is when I come to a word I don't know, I know how to take it on—I can sound it out, pronounce it. I can pick up a paper and read a lot more. I like papers, but I can only read some parts of them. But it's coming easier for me. I don't get frustrated. When I come to a word I don't know, I just work on it until I get it right.

I know for some people, it's hard to say they need help reading. They got too much pride to say that. But I ain't got too much pride to get help to learn something I want to do. You never know what people need help with unless you come and ask them. There's a lot of people out here who can't ask for help and don't want help. But I want help. I'm doing everything I can to better myself and improve my reading.

I tell people there's no harm in trying. And once you get into it, you'll see what you've been missing, what you can do, and then you'll say, I always *did* want to try this. I always *did* want to learn to read. And when you improve your reading, it will get you farther in the world, take you places you couldn't go before. Reading can get you from point A to point B, and maybe a lot of other places after B.

That's what I want from my reading—get to some of those other places. Get me a better job, maybe start a business. I want to sit down at night, read the paper, like that. I want to know what it say. I'm really proud of what I'm doing. I don't feel no shame about it. Why should I?

16. Hard to ask for help

The story of **Yolanda Gamble,** adult learner, Birmingham

GOD give everybody a different gift, and the gift of selling clothes went to my daddy. He worked at a store on Fourth Avenue here in Birmingham for many years. He sold suits, shirts, hats; he dressed them from head to toe. He was good at that, king of the kings, God bless his heart. And my mother worked at a chicken factory, chopping up chickens.

Growing up, I was mostly a homebody. I used to go to school, then come back home. I worked at home, living with my grandmother. I'd iron, cook, clean, go to the washers. I couldn't go nowhere with my friends, and I didn't have many friends. I wasn't allowed to go beyond the front porch. It was just me there; my brothers and sisters weren't with me. That was my life. Wasn't much of a childhood.

In school, they didn't know I had this reading problem. I just laughed and giggled with the rest of them. Some people know how to read, how to drive, but don't know how to play around it, you know? But I did. I played around it so my teachers didn't know I couldn't read. My family and a few friends did, but I hid it from the rest. When I got older, there were so many students in school the teachers didn't have time to help me. They kept me back a few years in school.

I always wanted to be a nurse. I think I always had a gift for that. When I was a kid, anybody got hurt, and my brothers were always getting hurt, I patched them up, fixed them up. There's a lot of things I wanted to do, but they didn't happen.

The person who helped me the most with my reading was the library teacher. She sat in the lunchroom with me every day for almost four years. She was the only one who had the time, or who took the time to help. She gave me the courage to go further. You know, a few years ago I ran into her; hadn't seen her in so many years. She invited me over to her house, and her house was just filled with books, shelves of books. Like a ship of books had just come in. It was amazing.

This reading program has helped a lot. I was just sitting at home before, trying to learn on my own, but then I came here. Got a good teacher here; Miss Tommie don't let us skip. She makes sure we show up, read the words, say the words, write the words. And she's teaching us just like you would a child coming up in elementary school.

One in seven adults in the U.S. lacks the literacy skills required to read anything more complex than a children's book, a staggering statistic that has not improved in more than 10 years.

— *Jessica Calefati, U.S. News & World Report*

This reading program gives me a reason to get out. Every morning I get up ready to come here, just like a job, and I like that. I can fill out applications for jobs now. I can understand a lot of what I see. I can say the right words in conversation. When I go in to fill out a job application now, I go in with my head up. My courage is up, too. Maybe I get the job, maybe I don't, but the thing is I know how to do it now. Our teacher here taught us a lot.

I'm looking for work right now. I can do a lot of things long as it don't involve computers, or babysitting! I've done a lot of jobs. I was a mechanic. I've done welding. I do cooking and cleaning sometimes. Drive trucks. I had some friends drove trucks all over the country. When they got tired, I'd drive: Arizona desert, California, Atlanta, New Orleans, and Texas, where my baby nephew was born. The places I been. I once drove from Texas to California, and from California back to Birmingham, in just two days.

I know it's hard for people who can't read to ask somebody for help: Lord, I know that. I went down that road. It's natural to fear that person you ask for help. And you don't feel you deserve it. When you're holding baggage between heaven and hell here on earth, you feel you don't deserve any help. You ain't about nothing. You never learned nothing. That's what you think, that's what your mind's telling you. In your mind, you can hear them laughing at you, talking about you. In your mind, they think you're nothing. They can't teach you nothing. You ain't ever learned a thing. So you're dealing with that fear, but you got to get your courage up; nobody laughing at you here.

Reading is a gift, so don't let it go, don't waste it. The Lord will guide you, so walk with him. It's like this about reading: I know a lot of people in this city who never been out of town, never been 50 miles from home. They don't even know their own city or state. They just go to work, go to the store, visit the mall, see a friend, come on home. Then do it all over again. They can't drive across town to a place just 15 or 20 minutes away without getting lost. They lived in town all their life but don't even know what's on the other side of the city or the state. Why? I'll tell you why: because they

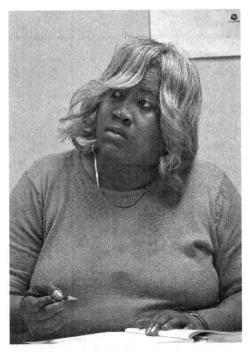

Yolanda Gamble says she became quite skilled in school at "playing around" her inability to read. That led to self-confidence issues. She notes that those who cannot read often limit themselves in so many other ways, including their ability to find their way around their own communities.

can't read streets. They can't read road numbers, can't read telephone numbers, can't read addresses. They don't want to go out to get lost, but they already lost because they can't read. Ain't that something?

17. Everything's a test

The story of **Tavarus Scott,** adult learner, Bessemer

I was born in Birmingham in 1985. I went to Jess Lanier High School and played football, basketball, baseball. Played sports most of my life for school, for church, just for fun. I still play a little softball at a park in Birmingham. I'd play some more football, too, if I could find the right team. I like to watch sports on TV, play video games, PlayStation. I like to play poker, shoot pool. I spend a lot of time on the computer.

Now I want to try to go back to school at Lawson State Community College to get me a skill, maybe paint and body work, auto technician, something like that. My goal is to improve my reading speed and comprehension so I can pass the test and get admitted to the program at Lawson. One day, I'd really like to open up a little paint and body shop. Have my own little business someday. And if that don't work out, maybe electronics.

I have one brother and one sister—actually three sisters. My mother adopted two of my cousins, but I call them my sisters. They're like sisters and live with us. One of them has a baby, and my sister has two babies. My little sister, she looks up to me. She stays with me 24/7. She watches everything I do. I try to live straight for her. My mom works for the police station in Bessemer, and my dad does landscaping work. My sister works at a day care center. When I finished high school I worked for the city of Bessemer for about two years. I'm working just a little bit right now.

Maybe the biggest family thing is this—one of my cousins shot another one of my cousins. That really smacked me, right there. I was 20 years old at the time. I heard they had an argument, and one shot the other. I was really upset, but then I cried it out. They just put my cousin on parole; he stays with me. I still hang with him. I don't really know what happened.

Freddie Fernandez, my stepbrother, went to the University of Alabama. He's into literacy. He's developed a little reading program in town, maybe a year ago. He works with youth who dropped out of school and who having trouble in school. He has a little house in town, just across from the Board of Education building, and invites the young people to come and study. They come in and work on computers, reading, writing; he wants to help them finish school. Four or five of his friends help him with the program. It's like a study group, you know? He's trying to get a grant for the program. Freddie's important to me, too. Help keep me straight, help push me to go to college.

> **The National Assessment of Adult Literacy (NAAL) showed adult prose literacy rates unchanged in the 2003 assessment versus 1992. Fourteen percent, or more than 30 million of U.S. adults, scored "below basic" in prose literacy.**
>
> — *National Center for Education Statistics*

My mom found out about this reading program, and she told me about it. I started reading here about two months ago. My tutor gave me the beginning books, and we started on those. But he said I didn't need those. I know how to sound out words, and I can read a bit. I know the vowels, and the letters, how to write the letters and words. I just need to learn to read faster to get into school so I can learn a trade. Dave Holt has me read some, and if there's a word I don't know, he makes me break it down, say it right and get the meaning. When I told him I wanted to read enough to pass the test at Lawson, he went out and got some practice tests. There's a little story or a couple of paragraphs at the top of the page, and then maybe 10 questions at the bottom that you have to answer. You have to comprehend the story to answer the questions. We're working on that. He thought that was a good way to prepare for the test.

I can already read more of the newspaper. I try to do that every day—read the whole sports section and then swing through the comics, see what they're saying. Reading better also helps my driving. When you go somewhere in Birmingham, there are little road signs, names and numbers. They're easier for me to understand now. And if you get lost, might have to tell somebody where you're at, and that's tough if you can't read the street signs and numbers.

Soon as I leave the reading session, I go get on the computer and read some more. I do a lot of reading on computer. I'm making progress. Every time I come here, I'm reading a little bit faster and I take away a couple new words.

At first it was hard to come and get help, ask somebody to help. I was embarrassed. But the thing that frustrates me the most now is how slow I read. I want to read faster, and I want to read faster today, not tomorrow or next year.

Way I see it, the world about reading because everything out here a test. You have to take a test to get a job. Take tests for school, for a diploma. Pass tests to get into college. Take a test to get a driver's license. Fill out forms and tests for insurance, medical things. I had to fill out an application for a job with the railroad. And I had to take a test on a computer for that job, too. World a series of tests, you know? You got to read to beat those tests.

18. A waitress has to read

The story of **Kayla Ann McGowan,** adult learner, Bessemer

I'M in this reading program because I want to go to college. But to get there I have to get a GED, see? So I'm at Lawson State working on that, and I've struggled a great deal with reading, so I asked if there was some place I could go for some reading help, and they directed me here to Dave Holt and the Bessemer Library program. So now I come to the library for about 90 minutes every day except Thursdays to work on my reading and math.

I'm learning how to read and build my vocabulary. When I read and come to words I don't understand, I write them on a sheet of paper and memorize what they mean. I'm starting to see some progress. I can read faster. I remember words better, and what they mean. So now I'm starting to get the whole story, see?

But finishing the GED is just my short-term goal. I want to continue reading. I'm a waitress, and a waitress has to be able to read and do math. So my longer term plan is to become an entrepreneur. I want to start a business like my grandparents' business; they own a café not far from here, just off exit #6 on the highway. I want to own and manage my own restaurant some day, like them. That's my dream. My grandparents raised me, and I saw how hard they worked. They also made money, and I want to work hard and make some money, too. I want the restaurant to be in Tennessee, up near Pigeon Forge. I think that's a beautiful area,

Highly self-motivated, Kayla Ann McGowan is working on her reading skills to get a GED and enter college. Currently a waitress, she dreams of owning her own restaurant in Tennessee. She says her daily 90-minute lessons at the Bessemer Library with Dave Holt always lift her spirits.

and I can see myself there, living and running a restaurant. I can really see that.

My grandmother is the biggest influence in my life. She disciplines me when I need that. She's also my biggest supporter and always there for me. She's there when my daddy and momma aren't there. She gave me a job at the café. She took care of me and got me what I needed. My momma would tell me she didn't have time to help me get it, but my grandmother would always help. She put me through school, too.

My twin sister's also important in my life. We're fraternal twins, but we look identical. We have these same thoughts, see? I mean, I can be thinking of something in my mind and then bang—my sister will just say it out loud! We do a lot of things together. We love going skating, and we're good at it. Skating is the biggest stress reducer for me.

When I was a child, I always wanted to do well in my reading and my math. But my momma didn't do well in school, and so she couldn't help me. So I decided I needed to take it on myself—learning to read. That's why I'm in this program, and I love it. The best thing is Mr. Holt—he always has a smile on his face. If I come here and I'm having a bad day, or if I'm upset about something, I always leave with a smile on my face. That's because of Mr. Holt. He has so much patience when I'm trying to learn words. He takes his time and helps me out with problems, like understanding a word, or how to sound it out. I always leave the reading sessions with a good, upbeat attitude.

The annual high school dropout rate in the U.S. remains at about 33 percent.

— *The Education Trust*

The best thing about learning to read is that it makes me feel great! I'm excited. I can read in front of others now and not be so nervous or so hesitant to speak up. I can spell it out for them. And I love that feeling. It's like having a power I didn't have before, and I love it.

And in the restaurant, I can write the words for the orders, and I can do the math and add up the bills. I really struggled with that before. But now they even let me run the cash register!

19. My tutor always showed up

The story of **Baron Martin,** teenage learner,
Bessemer

I was born in Washington, D.C., and moved here
when I was nine. My mom wanted to get out of D.C.
and come down here to Alabama to see what it was
like. So she came here and bought a house; it's the first
house I ever lived in. My sister lives here with me and
my mom. Three other siblings live back in D.C.

I'm in the seventh grade, and I have classes in
math, language, social studies, science and reading. I
like language the best because I can write—essays,
poems, stuff like that. I like to write. And I like music:
piano sometimes, quiet music. And the old music: the
Ojays, Whispers, Maxwells, soft music, you know.

I want to play football for Alabama. I'm playing this
year in eighth grade, my first year. I'm a running back.
I've always loved football. One of my uncles played pro
football for the Washington Redskins: Eddie "Flash"
Martin. Maybe you know him. He played in the late
70s, or early 80s. And my physical education teacher at
the school I went to in D.C., he played pro football,
too, with the Redskins. His name is Eddie Field.

Football and family are the two most important
things in my life. I'm very protective of family. Some
people don't have families, but I'm a lucky one who
does. I want to protect my family. And I do what I can
to help mom out. When I get money, I give some of it
to mom.

My mother and my tutor, Robert, have inspired me
a lot. My mom's a tough lady; she's been through a lot.

She's close friends with me, and she's an independent woman. She's very smart and intelligent—and very pretty. What I've learned from her is that when it's tough around you, you have to make everything work. She says, when you only have a little bit left, you have to learn to work with what you have.

Robert tells me I can read better, and I believe in him. We've been working together for about five months. When I struggle with a word, he thinks of another word, just about like it, that I might know. Then we talk about it and mix the two words up a bit, and then I understand it and can pronounce it. He helps me sound out words. Right now we're reading two books: the *Fantastic Mr. Fox* and the Bible. I like to read the Bible. My great grandfather was a minister, and so was one of my uncles. And there's another in the family who's studying to be a minister, so we have some family members in the church.

> **The standards for literacy achievement keep rising.... The knowledge skills and the communication systems they ride along all change even faster than children do.**
>
> — *Deborah Brandt, Literacy and Learning*

I'm reading better now. I made some progress. I understand more words, and I'm reading faster. I comprehend more. There's a bigger book I've wanted to read for awhile; it's one of my goals. The book is called *Trapped in a President's Body*. It's about three friends who were going to school, and they heard that the president was going to visit their school. But then the president fell, and one of their friends fell, and they were in comas, and when they woke up they were in each other's body. I know it sounds like a crazy story, but I'm going to read it.

The most important thing for me is to believe that I can do this—that I can get it together and read books. My tutor gives me confidence. When I first started I didn't really think I could do it, and I was nervous. But Robert gave me confidence, and I started to trust him. You know why? Because he always showed up. That's it. Whenever I'd come, and sometimes I'd come early, he was always here. He was always in this room, waiting for me. He showed up in my life. Me and him have become best friends. He's like family. Me and him have both come from a rough life, so we have that in common. And AD problems, we have that, too. He know what problems I'm having with the reading. He had them, too.

One of my friends is having trouble with reading, just like me. I told him about Robert—that he's a good tutor for teenagers who don't know how to read. So he was thinking about talking to Robert, and now he and his mom are coming in a couple of weeks to meet my tutor and get started learning. I said maybe he could come and sit in on a session with me, see how it goes. So I already recruited one person to learn how to read.

In my old school in D.C., they didn't really help me with my reading. They didn't even care. But when we got here, I saw some information about this program, and I signed up for it. I want to read more. I want to read better. And I need to read for when I get older. When I become a pro football player, I have to be able to read my contracts, you know? If I didn't come here for this reading help, and if I didn't improve my reading, I might sign a contract with things in it I don't know nothing about.

So I want to be able to read my own contracts in football, and everything else that's important in my life or my family's life. My mom explained that life can be hard, but it can be harder if you don't know how to read, or how to do that math. People might take advantage of you. I'm learning to read so that don't happen to me.

20. Hang with good people

The story of **Steven Gilbert,** adult learner, Tuscaloosa

I try hard to stay out of trouble and stay out of jail. I want to improve myself. I'm in the reading program in Tuscaloosa to restart my education so I can own my own business someday. I want my own home, a car, a girl, some kids and my own money, if it ain't too much to ask. And I want to be able to support my father and mother—help them pay bills and any little thing they might need help with, like keeping the house clean, the yard clean, put some money in their pocket, too.

Right now I'm looking for a job. Couple years ago I worked at Sonic Drive In, but not for long. Sometimes I do a little lawn work. Cut some grass or do some yard clean up. Maybe wash some cars. Weekends I teach Sunday school with little kids, 5-6 years old. I read some scripture to them. They get up in front of the church, and I ask them questions. They're fun.

> **Twenty percent of high school seniors can be classified as being functionally illiterate at the time they graduate.**
>
> — *Education-Portal.com, July 24, 2007*

I went to Central High School in Tuscaloosa. At Shelton State, I'm trying to pass a reading test to get into the GED program. When I finish the GED, I want to go into an auto mechanics program, but I got to pass the test for that.

I want my own business someday—an auto body shop. That's my dream right now.

Steven Gilbert has his sights on the American Dream—with a home, car, family and his own auto body shop. But first he needs to earn his GED at Shelton State. Strongly influenced by his grandmother, he reminds himself daily of her mantra to keep out of trouble and to stay focused on his goals.

I want to work on the panels and fix dents, accident repairs. Maybe I can have some people work for me. My brothers and uncles do some bodywork now. I hang with them a lot; they teaching me how to do this and do that—change a tire, change brakes and rotors, do a motor job, stuff like that. They teaching me how to get ready for the day when I complete my GED.

My grandmother helped me a lot in life. She get me to school and take me to the movies. She cook for us on weekends. She give me lots of advice. Like, don't get caught up in trouble, or mess with anybody. Be a leader not a follower. Told me to do what my parents told me to do, don't talk back. Follow their rules because they love me. She said some people on the street, they ain't love me like my parents do.

Stay away from trouble, she told me. Don't hang with the wrong people, and don't look for trouble. Don't hang around people who want to hurt others, or kill somebody. Don't be robbing, stealing, killing, all those things. Don't hang with people looking for conflicts with other people all the time.

All these things she tell me, over and over, you know? I can still hear her. She inspired me. There's lots of trouble everywhere, least where I grew up, so you got to stay away from it. Sometimes it ain't easy because trouble hang on every street and corner, you know? One of my cousins called me up one time and wanted me to go with him, beat up somebody. Said this guy done bad to him. But I told him, I wasn't going. I didn't want the trouble. I ain't never been in jail, I ain't never been in juvenile, and I told him I ain't trying to go that way. I don't want to sit and waste my life in jail. I want to have my own business and a home and a family. I want to read to help me do all that.

Miss Chancy asked me if I wanted to join a reading class at Shelton State. She told me that I had to make a 6.0 or higher to get into the GED program. She said the PLUS program could help me do that. That sparked me. I went through some one-on-one tutoring here at the library for about four months, you know? And I was tutored for four or five months at Shelton State. Now I go to this reading class three days a week for about three hours each day.

We're working on test scores, comprehension, how to pronounce words, antonyms, synonyms, the meaning of words in context, stuff like that. The teacher helps a lot. He comes around and works with each one of us and writes things on the board and explains them to us.

My reading has improved, for sure. My tutors show me how to break words down, do the sounds, make some meaning. Book I'm working in now helps me understand how to fill out an application for a job, step-by-step: How to fill out your work history, how to prepare for a job interview, how to dress for an interview, how to show up neat and be on time, stuff like that to get you a job.

I read the newspaper and the Bible every morning. I look for jobs in the newspaper and then I read some scripture. Reading help you improve your life. That's what I believe, you know? You got to read to get a job, get ahead. That's what I learned. And you need help to do that, so I'm getting some help. I don't want to hang with the wrong people and end up in jail.

Stories of Discovery

Coming to engage

21. Don't be afraid

The story of **Cheryl Moon,** adult learner,
Birmingham

I never really knew my father, just his name. I was
born in Birmingham and went to Phillips High
School, in special education. I want to learn to read so I
can work in day care or be a tutor. I don't have any
children, but I'd like to work with them. Some children
need help, and I could make a difference.

I'd like to be a writer and be able to tell others
about learning to read so that they aren't afraid to try.
I'd like to help them be less afraid. I know if you can't
read, you afraid of words. I was.

My family and friends encouraged me to go on and
try to learn to read. You can do it, they say. They help
me. They give me courage. Sometimes I feel down
about my reading. It's so hard. But my friends keep
encouraging me. Don't down yourself, they say. Keep
on. So I keep on trying.

Church is the center of my life. I go to Mt. Mariah
Baptist Church, and I sing in the choir. I've gone to
that church for a long time. I like it because the people
are very nice. They help me do things. They show love
to me, kindness. The pastor and his wife are so nice. I
want to learn to read so I can help others, and so I can
read the Bible in church. I'd like to read to others.
Reading and words help us, don't they?

Two people are really important in my life: my pastor's wife and Miss Tommie. They show me love. They
encourage me. They care for me. I been working on my

Being able to read Bible stories to others in church drives Cheryl Moon to pursue her lessons with "Miss Tommie." She notes her steady progress by her increasing ability to read package labels while shopping. Eventually she wants to become a tutor herself.

reading for about a year, and Miss Tommie show me the way. She a fine lady.

I want to better myself by reading. It's coming slow, but in my daily life I can read more in my Bible. The words is coming more clearly, and I love the little stories in the Bible. I can read more in grocery stores, too. I can read the labels on the cans and boxes, what's in them and then decide to buy or not. I just guessed what was in them before, or I just always bought what I always bought.

How to get people like me started with reading, that's the hard part. I guess I would tell them my experience, how I started, how you can come forward for help. I would tell them don't be afraid to talk to someone, you can do it. My life here can be an example. You don't have to be afraid to learn.

And I would tell them if they want to read, I will bring them here to the Literacy Council. I will let them talk to Miss Tommie. She a good teacher. She will welcome you and go through the books with you. She has shown me things and taught me things I didn't think I could read. But she led the way for me. She can lead the way for you, too. Don't be afraid. Don't be ashamed. You can do it.

22. The little rock that starts the ripple

The story of **Louise Crow,** University of Alabama graduate student and president, Literacy is the Edge

I come from a big southern family that lives in the Mobile area, and my family and faith have shaped my values. My parents always held me and my brother accountable for our own decisions. My dad comes from a very hardworking background, he paid his way through college and today he owns an accounting and financial planning firm. He instilled a strong work ethic in us and the belief that education is the key to success. Always give 100 percent to everything you do—that's his motto. I remember when my brother was in high school and wasn't doing that well, my dad sent him to work in a tough construction job for a summer. That was his way of emphasizing the importance of education to my brother.

My mother's hard working, too, but she has this wonderful, zany side. She's just so much fun to be around. She's a cancer survivor, and she always sees the good side to everything; live life to the fullest is what she says, and that's what she does. She's personable, loves learning about others and is a great inspiration to her family and her friends.

Like her, I love to have fun, too. Growing up on Mobile Bay, water was really part of our culture. We do water sports, boating, fishing, celebrate holidays on the water, all that. I played sports in high school, and I was the female Rudy, you know? Never the fastest, never the most athletic, but I worked hard and put my heart and soul into every practice and every game. Now I enjoy running; I ran a half marathon in Nashville this

Instilled with a strong work ethic and the importance of education, Louise Crow talks about the "chill" she experienced when introduced to the opportunity to become a tutor. Later, as head of the university's student program, LITE, she helped recruit hundreds of students to serve as tutors in the region.

spring. I had no running experience, but I finished it and there was this incredible rush, just this wonderful high from accomplishment.

When I heard about the student group Literacy is the Edge, or LITE, it was a chill bump for me. It really struck a nerve. I wanted to be involved with this organization and have the opportunity to become part of something new and help someone read. What could be finer than that? It still sends chills down my spine.

Literacy also is an issue that I knew so little about—the depth and scope of the problem and how much it affected Alabama economically and socially. Most people are unaware that one in four Alabamians are functionally illiterate.

What I take away from my experience as president of LITE this year is just this: It is the most rewarding experience I've ever had in any service learning class, organization or leadership role. Being part of something new and helping build it made it even better. We also got to combine a communications skill set we had and were developing with a real need in the community. So we planned and carried out this campaign to recruit UA students to become reading tutors in the community. We learned by doing and by doing something important.

I think we truly made a small difference in some lives around us. I mean, think about it: We recruited nearly 800 UA students as volunteers, and then 250 of them were trained as tutors who then went to work with children and adults in the local community. Wow! There's a ripple effect that will help others see the magnitude of the problem; then they will want to tell their friends and get involved, and some of their friends will get involved, and so forth. It's a tremendous feeling to be part of the little rock that starts that ripple, part of that small wave that gets people our age involved throughout the community. It's an experience of a lifetime for me.

One of my most memorable experiences with LITE was our first tutor training session, which took place at Shelton State Community College. It was in the late afternoon, and there was a traffic tie-up that blocked access to the college. So when I finally made it into the college, there were only five or six people in the audience. That's when I started to get sweaty palms and I thought, oh-oh, maybe it won't work. Maybe we didn't reach the students after all because nobody was there!

Then, one by one, the students began showing up, and they all apologized for being late because of the traffic. And though we started about 45 minutes late, more than 50 students showed up that first evening for the training. And then everyone introduced themselves and expressed what literacy meant to them and why they wanted to help others learn to read. Every answer was different, but every answer was just so incredibly heartfelt. Every person had a powerful story to tell, and their passion was so real. To see that so many young people cared about that issue, well, I will never forget that night. We had started something really good, something really important.

> **Nearly one in six Alabamians—and one in four of our children—live below the federal poverty line, which is $21,203 in household earnings for a family of four.**
>
> — *Alabama Poverty Project*

I'm tutoring an elementary child now, a young girl. I was so nervous when I first met her. I didn't know what level she was reading at, or if I would be able to help her. But she's such a sweet girl. I meet her in the school library, and she reads better than I thought. The biggest thing is she lacks confidence in her own ability. She had a fear of reading aloud in front of others. That took me back to my own childhood because I used to get really nervous and tried to fly through the sentences when I had to read aloud in front of others.

So I'm helping her work through that. She's moved from being shy and reading softly to where she is more animated and confident. She's also moved up her overall reading level in her grade. What it seemed to take was just having someone spend time with her, listen to her, and give her some confidence. She already had the skill set: She just needed to prove it to herself. It's a wonderful thing to see. It's the best part of each week for me; everything else in my life just goes away when I'm with her.

I've learned that literacy is the central root for many social and economic issues that we confront: crime, poverty, unemployment, high school dropout rates, you name it. Reading is such a crucial key. I believe every little bit helps, and everyone can help just a little bit. You can make others aware. You can become a tutor. You can see someone having difficulties in the grocery store, and you can help them out. Please, just give a little bit; it will make a difference. Everyone in Alabama and the world should be able to read and enjoy the rich possibilities that come with understanding written words.

23. It's just overwhelming

The story of **Mary Lena Morgan,** adult tutor,
Tuscaloosa

MY parents met in an ESL class in Mexico. After
my father graduated from the University of
Alabama, he went to Mexico to teach ESL classes. They
met in one of those classes and were married there.
Dad then went to law school in Idaho, and we moved
around for a bit, Oregon and a couple of other places,
before returning to Tuscaloosa. I went to Holy Spirit
Elementary School here in town and then attended a
private high school in Birmingham. I earned a B.A. in
psychology at Trinity College in Connecticut. Now I'm
27 and have a two-year-old daughter.

After college, I worked in an after-school program
for kids in Charleston, South Carolina. Then I returned
here and worked in a doctor's office for about a year.
Now I'm thinking about returning to school to earn a
graduate degree in educational psychology, or maybe
social work. My husband just took a job in Nashville,
and we'll be moving there in a couple of months. I'm
exploring both degrees at UT Nashville, and will wait
until we're relocated to decide.

When I have time with my daughter, we do things
together—go to the playground, the Children's Hands
on Museum, the library. I want her to do things to
enrich her life. I was more active before becoming a
mom. I liked kayaking, backpacking, hiking and so
forth. I also love to read, and that's something that got
me interested in tutoring, along with some experiences
I had in Canada and South Africa. They built my confi-

dence and pushed me to get involved in the larger world out there.

I took a National Outdoors Leadership Program in college. It's a lot like Outward Bound. You go out for 45 days, you learn a lot of outdoor skills and you develop leadership skills to use in the real world. What I took away from that experience was the importance of competency—being able to rely on yourself, and being able to let people rely on you. It's great to have support and be able to call on people when you need support, but I came away from there realizing that I wasn't helping myself by letting other people do things for me. I needed to be more self-reliant even as I learned the value of a support group.

Two-thirds of the world's illiterate adults are women.

— ProLiteracy, 2010

The program was held in the Yukon in Canada. We backpacked the first half of the trip and canoed the second half. It was great to get all the noise out of your life—all the stuff going on that you carry around in civilization. I was in a group of 11 people I didn't know. Whether you like everyone in the group or don't, you learn to rely on them. And you can't backslide. In a small group in the wilderness, your interpersonal skills come into play. I learned so much about myself that summer and gained a lot of confidence.

My six-week trip to South Africa one summer was another incredible experience. I went for a summer study program in human rights. Just going there for a couple of months you can't say that you understand it, or that you have fully experienced it, but it is eye opening to see the poverty, the inequality. It's stunning. I know we have that in this country, too, but in South Africa, it was so immediate, so intense, so fresh. We were immersed in it. When I returned from that trip, I was much more aware of some of the social and historical inequalities in our lives and the hardships that some people face every day.

I became involved in tutoring when I saw information about the adult education and literacy program at Shelton State Community College. It was among a list of organizations with which students could get involved. At the time I was applying to be a substitute teacher, and I was already volunteering at the Catholic Social Services Agency in town, so I thought this would be something I would enjoy that would have a positive impact. I mean, I love to read. I don't know what my life would be like if I couldn't read. Reading is one of my passions, and being able to share that with someone who hasn't had the opportunities to learn would be a rewarding experience. Maybe it could make a difference.

> **Low health literacy costs between $106 billion and $238 billion each year in the United States.**
>
> — *ProLiteracy, 2010*

My adult learner is a retired widow, aged 75, who wants to gain her GED. She's been interested in this for a while, and she tried some GED prep classes before, but they moved too fast for her. So she became involved with the PLUS program at Shelton State to improve her reading ability and prepare for the GED. She dropped out of school when she was in eighth grade, so obtaining a GED is her personal goal. She wants to do it for herself. She wants to climb that mountain.

She's still a very active, very healthy woman who volunteers to help other elderly people in the community who need some assistance. And she wants to find a part-time job, which is hard to do without a GED. Her main problem with reading is comprehension. She can read many words but has difficulty understanding and comprehending meaning. She also has difficulty understanding more complex writing—things like multiple choice questions on GED tests, which are more about analysis and subtle differences in meaning.

We started out using material provided by the PLUS program, but she felt the reading was too easy and the questions weren't preparing her for the GED. So I began supplementing the readings with having her write in a journal and bring in reading materials that interested her. She likes to read the newspaper, for example, and she's interested in cooking. We went through a period of time where we were mutually frustrated with the materials and what we were trying to achieve. We were trying to find the right balance— what was challenging but not too challenging. We also learned to relate to each other because of these difficulties in finding the right balance. That was a big discovery for me: learning and teaching, it's a two-person process. I needed to not just teach her how to do something, but I also needed to learn *how* to teach her. You know what I'm saying?

What I hope she carries away from this experience is that her goal is reachable. I hope she continues to believe that and continue with her study. I hope she doesn't become frustrated with it and give up. I hope she will continue. We spent a lot of time working on the multiple-choice questions, how to approach the questions, strategies to eliminate the clearly wrong answers, and so forth. I hope those skills stay with her.

The literacy problem is truly overwhelming. I see it so many places. I spend a lot of volunteer time at the Catholic Social Services Agency, where people come for food and financial assistance. Or maybe they are going to have their power cut off, or they face eviction—real living problems. When people come in to request financial assistance, they have to fill out a form about their income, their expenses, the reasons they are unable to pay and so forth. Most of the people need help filling out the entire form because they can't read enough to complete the forms on their own. It's very rare that they don't exhibit reading or writing problems, grammatical issues, spelling. It's such a struggle for them just to complete the forms to get some help.

And doesn't that struggle suggest something about what kind of life is available to you without reading skills? What your choices are and how big the limitations are? I can't imagine what I would do if I couldn't read. I know people find ways of coping with it, and there are probably more safety nets and supportive groups in our society than ever to help them. But the need is so great, so overwhelming. You see it in the social service agencies, public schools, grocery stores, churches, communities. It's just overwhelming.

24. New jobs, new perspectives

The story of **Grant Hiatt,** administrative assistant,
The Literacy Council in Birmingham

I had a hard time finding a paying job in 2004 after I graduated from the University of Alabama, where I majored in philosophy and minored in creative writing, so I've done some different things. I first worked just down the street on First Avenue at the Church of the Reconciler, a homeless shelter, where they had what they call a restorative justice program.

Homeless people incur a lot of fines; it's just part of their lifestyle. They have to trespass just to find someplace to stay. They have to go to the bathroom outside, for which they receive public indecency citations. And when they get all of these fines, they can't pay them so they wind up in jail. This homeless shelter had a program where people could do community service instead of fines, and they needed someone to administer the program. That's what I did for about a year. I became a notary public so that I could get their consent to complete their background forms, and I accompanied them to court and documented their community service hours.

Then I got a job as a hydraulic dredge operator in the bio waste management field, dredging and dewatering municipal waste. I did that for about three years up and down the West Coast in Oregon and Washington, northern California. That was an 80-hour a week job, which got old after a few years, so I came back here and started working for the Literacy Council in 2008, first through the Vista AmeriCorps program and then, when they had an opening here, as a part-time administrator.

For the future, I have an application in at Auburn University for a professional technical writing program. That appeals to me because it's just another way to do a lot more different things. Other than that, the only long-term dream I have is to someday take the Foreign Service exam. I'm trying to improve my Spanish and become a candidate for that. Then I could go somewhere else in the world and do more different things. I'm driven to try out new things.

All of these experiences have been important in terms of how I see the world and who I am. When I worked for Synagro, the bio-solids management company on the West Coast, I was a project manager and dredge operator. I operated a lot of machines, worked with a variety of people, and changed my perspective from what I had in college. I don't know everybody's mindset when they leave college, but I came out of college feeling like I was smarter than a lot of other people. But when I couldn't find a paying job, it was humbling, to say the least.

Then I went to work in this strange, manual labor job, dredging waste, and I first viewed these crazy roughnecks I worked with as savage and ignorant people. But it turns out they are cultured in the strangest ways, they're super intelligent, they're very talented, and they became my best friends during those three years. This experience gave me a much better perspective on the world and the different people in it. I also worked with a lot of people from the Pacific Islands and Mexico.

All of these mad men were foodies. The guys from the islands would make fish tartar dishes; guys from the south would slow cook chicken neck bones. They were all unpretentious about the aesthetic aspects of things like that, gourmet cooking. But they did it really well, they savored it, and I learned to savor it, too. For some reason, dredging waste broadened my mind in ways that a college education didn't.

I had a reverse kind of experience when I lived in San Francisco. I'd always thought of SF as a liberal, cultured place, but the people I met there had no appreciation for the people I met at Synagro. I would bring people from that industry I knew into the city, and vice versa, and I always found that my friends in SF were hostile to my other friends in Synagro and critical about what I did in general. That changed my perspective on people and made me appreciate Alabama a lot more. I guess SF was too liberal and cultured. I felt like George Wallace out there, and here I feel like Abby Hoffman. You know what I mean?

> **If the world were a village of only 100 people, 67 of them would be adults, and half of them would be illiterate.**
>
> — *State of the Village Report*

My dad has done many things in his life, and he's inspired me. He's always encouraged me to try to go down different paths, and to use my resourcefulness in different situations. He thinks this makes you a more complete person. He studied biology in college, and when he graduated he was drafted into the army. He was trained to be a radio operator, but then he went to Ft. Hood, Texas, where they put him to work with the GED program for soldiers in the stockade there. After that, he started teaching biology in Camden, Arkansas, where he met my mom. They were married and moved to Memphis, where he taught biology some more. Then they moved to Columbia, Missouri, where he studied to be a respiratory therapist. It was Charlotte, South Carolina, after that, where he sold medical supplies for Kimberly Clark. Then we came to Birmingham, where he became CEO of the Visiting Nurse Association. He subsequently started his own geriatric clinic with a partner, a doctor. Then, after he retired, he started his own gas field services company in Arkansas. You can see he's a man who doesn't sit still for long.

I came to literacy and tutoring in the same naïve way that a lot of people do, I imagine. I saw the job posting, a coordinator position, and I thought, oh, literacy, I like to read, I'll do that! You know. And when people call now to volunteer, they say the same thing—I like to read, I would like to be a reading tutor. I was literally that naïve. That was in 2008. I talked to Steve Hannum, and he encouraged me. I went through some training, and then I started as a generally unsuccessful literacy coordinator in Shelby County. I don't know anything about community organizing, but it was a good learning experience.

In my tutoring I've worked with some fascinating adults. Anthony was one of them. He'd worked previously as a concrete demolitions specialist, where he operated by remote control a really sophisticated eight-legged spider robot. It would crawl or go into places unsafe for humans to chip concrete. He'd been trained to use this very sophisticated robot, and he knew that he was vulnerable given his limited reading abilities. So he wanted to protect his job, and he never trained anyone else to use the robot.

But one day he fell off a water tower and broke his back. It took him a long time to recuperate, and he lived with a great deal of pain and just couldn't do the robot job any more. Because he couldn't read, he was unable to land another job. But he was a very talented mechanic, and he told me that if he could get his reading up to speed, then he thought he could become a certified mechanic.

We worked for about a year in Shelby County before he eventually moved away to Mississippi. I remember the first few sessions we worked together before I had completed my tutor training—I didn't really know what I was doing. So we wrote out the alphabet, and that was no problem. And then I said we could start to work on letters, and start with the vowels, and he said that's exactly what he wanted to learn. He had a high degree of word recognition, but he had a really tough time with words he hadn't seen before, or that didn't pronounce phonetically quite the way they looked like they should.

Two good things happened during that year together. First, Anthony improved his reading. But even more, he began to grow into the habit of reading. We have some good Bibles here that are made for low literacy people, and I gave him one of those, and he led some Sunday school classes at his church in their readings. He was very proud of that.

Alma was another student, a really great person who called us and wanted a place where she could study for the GED. She's about 60, and a lot of the courses at the community colleges are filled with young people, and they're computer-based programs, which she's uncomfortable with. So I asked her if she would like me to be her tutor for the GED. We did a lot of literacy and reading work, as well as a lot of math. She works in a custodial job now, and part of her longer-term goal is to find a different job.

It meant a lot to me with both students that we wound up becoming good friends. It can't be helped in tutoring. Maybe it's a natural thing because you spend so much time together and you talk about life. They don't have anyone in their life quite like me, and I don't have anyone in my life quite like each of them, so whenever we got together we were quite interested in each other.

One thing I noticed in both students is that they have amnesia when it comes to the progress they've made since we started. And I can see why because no matter where we go in terms of progress, they still have a long way to go to master reading and comprehension. But they never notice how far they've come. One way I deal with this is to travel back to the past. I literally flip back the pages and ask them, do you remember how hard this was and now how easy it is for you? Today we did something you once told me you could never do, but now you can. And today you tell me you can't do something, but you can. And in the future we will look back and see that you did do it.

There's just no way that adult tutoring can compete with reading education at a young age in school. Reading education is the best way to conquer illiteracy. At the same time, adult tutoring is very important, and it's something that many people want. I'm not sure how to make that process any more efficacious or efficient, other than getting more people involved as tutors. To that end, more people in the community need to be more aware of the big problem that illiteracy is in the community.

When I worked with Anthony and Alma, I found them to be interesting and intriguing people, but they saw themselves as unintelligent. I hate that. I try to convince them otherwise and make the analogy between reading and any kind of skill. Like anything, it's much easier to do when you're young, but it's also possible to do when you are older. With Alma, she didn't learn to drive a car until she was 45 or 50. So I use that analogy with her and say, look, most people learn to drive when they're 16, but you already know it wasn't impossible to do when you were older. It's the same thing with reading—easier when you're younger, but not impossible when you are older. You learn to drive a car, you learn to read. And just because you can't read as well as you want yet, it doesn't mean you aren't intelligent. It just means you never learned how, not yet. Like driving a car, or playing a piano.

I try to build up their confidence. I actually try to downplay how important reading is; I play it up as just one of many skills we use every day, one more skill. That seems to help them get a better perspective on it, get up some confidence. And I think that's true: One of the main reasons for reading is to help with many practical aspects of our lives. I can't imagine life without reading.

25. Make a difference

The story of **Lauren Radziminski,** junior, University of Alabama

I became aware of the literacy program in fall 2008 when two students came and spoke to the Honors College about Literacy is the Edge, the student group on campus. I went with a friend to one of the tutoring sessions. When I learned that so many children and adults struggled with reading and writing, I decided I needed to commit to doing something about this. I wanted to help. If I can have the opportunity to gain a higher education, then all children should at least have the opportunity to be able to learn to read and write.

I'm majoring in international relations and minoring in French and general business, and I'm involved in campus and community activities because it's important to be engaged in the world. For example, I'm the president of the business fraternity, Alpha Kappa Psi. We hold professional events and teach students how to prepare résumés and prep for interviews. I also serve as an ambassador for the Honors College and participate in the Save First Tax Initiative in Tuscaloosa. We help lower income families prepare their taxes, free of charge.

I think my commitment to community grows out of three strong and wonderful women who have influenced my life. My mom is first on that list. One of the most powerful experiences for me came when my parents divorced. For 10 years after that my mom was a single parent. It was the prime of my young life, from about age 8-18, so growing up with a single parent, see-

Lauren Radziminski has been strongly influenced by three very independent women in her family, from whom she learned the importance of being "engaged with the world." She observes that tutoring can be both frustrating and rewarding as she tries to determine how best to reach and motivate different students.

ing everything that she had to do, wow! Mom would drive me to school, pick me up, drive me everywhere, and still pursue a challenging career with long days in the office. She's very independent, very strong willed, and always achieving things others thought she couldn't. I think I'm just as strong as she is, and I know I wouldn't have made it this far if I wasn't. She's given me so much and been such a role model.

Another significant experience came during my last two years of high school. My mom remarried, and my stepdad's cousin was a former ambassador to Kenya, a really remarkable lady. She became the whole reason I wanted to study international relations. I always thought I was going to be a dance major, but when I talked with her and learned about everything she's done in Kenya—and she also was the ambassador to Guatemala—it was so exciting and challenging. She broadened my horizons and vision tremendously, and I told myself that's what I want to do: Get involved and make a difference.

My grandmother in Pittsburgh is the third woman—she gave me a deep appreciation for family. She has 14 brothers and sisters, and her parents are from Poland, and I'm so impressed with her because she still keeps in touch with all of her living brothers and sisters. Since I'm an only child, having a huge family of relatives is wonderful.

> **The saddest casualties of illiteracy in America are the children who are affected by intergenerational illiteracy.**
>
> — *Washington County Literacy Council*

We always have a vigil dinner on Christmas Eve. My grandmother puts it together, and it takes her about two weeks to prepare. Then she feeds 30 people—aunts, uncles, kids, grandkids, cousins—every Christmas Eve before we go to Mass. My grandmother has a really small house, so it's a challenge hosting 30 people. But having a family that's deeply rooted in tradition—and her family used to do the vigil dinner, and before that her grandparents did it—is really important to me. I want to be able to do that after she passes. She's 86 now, and she still does it all. It's so important to her to have all of her family together, for one day each year, to celebrate the tradition and each other. To me it's amazing and inspiring. I know we live in an age when some people are shaking off traditions, but I don't want to. The vigil dinner has great meaning for me, and I want to keep it alive.

So these three women have had a lot to do with my involvement, including tutoring. After my tutor training, I was placed in Holt Elementary School with three third-graders—two boys and a girl. The girl wanted to improve so much; she had that "let's do this" attitude. I would read my book to her first, and then she would have one of her books to read. She read much slower than I expected, no more than four or five words a minute, so it was difficult for her to get through the material. Some of the words she knew, but many were new. And whenever she was writing her sentences about which book she liked the most, she struggled with it. She'd get stuck on harder words like "friend" and "because," larger words for her. But she understood many verbs, and small words like "I" and "we" and "the."

She improved a lot during the semester and began to read faster and recognize more words. But with writing, and this was a problem for all three of my students, she would write down a new word, and spell it back to me, but when it came time for the next session, she didn't remember the new word. She forgot it during the course of a week.

My second student was a boy, but I only tutored him a few weeks. His family pulled him out of school and sent him to another elementary school. He had the most struggles. He couldn't put together the correct sounds to actually say the words aloud. He could only get basic words down like "I" and "we," one-syllable words. Writing was also very difficult for him, even the simplest words. The sad thing is, he was in his normal grade level, grade three, and probably falling further behind every day.

The last student was a boy, too, a real firecracker. He was very jumpy and couldn't sit down or sit still. He didn't seem to care that his reading and writing weren't up to par, and it was difficult just to get him to try to read. He lacked the motivation to read, and I struggled to find ways to motivate him.

But there were some wonderfully positive moments, too. One of the biggest moments for my little girl came when she wrote her paragraph about her story without having to ask for any help. She was really happy with that. I said, "You wrote that all by yourself. You didn't need any help!" And she said, "I really did it, didn't I?" Like she couldn't believe it. She had the biggest smile.

For the boy, I remember especially the day that he got through an entire book without having to ask for help, without making a mistake. Most days he'd have to ask me what something meant, or what is it, you know, what does that word say? But that day he read the entire book, no mistakes, and no help. Talk about smiles!

Overall, I was excited to tutor them. I hope I improved their lives just a little bit. I hope with their improved reading and writing skills that they will go further in life and enjoy it more. I hope they succeed in whatever place their lives take them to. Maybe college, or going to work in a job they want, or helping other people down the road with the skills that I helped them with. I know it's just a small thing, but it meant a lot to me to be with them.

Given the size of the reading problem in Alabama, we need more tutors in the schools. I worked with three children, several times a week, and they needed more help than I could give them. Many kids in elementary and middle school could benefit from one-on-one reading help. I wasn't even aware of the problem before. When I went home to Huntsville last summer, my friends asked about some of the things I did at college, and I started talking about Literacy is The Edge. I had the paperwork with all of the facts that the students gave us, and I showed them the brochure. They just had no idea. They had no clue that functional illiteracy touched nearly one in four people in Alabama. So we need to make this issue a lot more visible.

26. Let's be #1 in reading

The story of **Dave Holt,** tutor and coordinator,
Ready to Read Program, Bessemer Public Library

I grew up in International Falls, Minnesota, a mill town that is famous as the coldest spot in the U.S. in winters. I think my elementary school teachers and the librarian set up my whole life. They helped me to learn to read and to enjoy what I could gain from books and the classroom. I learned to be a good student and a good reader in elementary school, which helped lead me to an appointment at the U.S. Air Force Academy.

I graduated from the academy, became a pilot and was commissioned in 1962. I retired in 1986, flying about half of my career. One of my early assignments was quite memorable. We flew rescue missions out of Okinawa, and we'd often land on local islands to pick up people who had problems. The three main problems were snakebites, pregnancy complications, or appendicitis, and they always seemed to happen about 2 a.m. We'd find our way to these islands through someone lighting a bonfire in the middle of a baseball field; there seemed to be a ball field on every island. Then we'd land and meet with people who spoke nothing but Japanese—a crew full of people who only spoke English met with a group of people who only spoke Japanese. Think about that!

This led me to study Japanese, and I earned an M.A. in Asian Studies and became an Asian specialist in the Air Force. I spent eight years in Japan and three years in the Pentagon as a Japan specialist. After retiring from the Air Force, my wife and I settled in Atlanta,

After a career in the U.S. Air Force, where he became a Japanese specialist, Dave Holt retired to teach math and then moved to Alabama. He started the literacy program in Bessemer, quickly aligning new students to tutors who can also serve as a life coach. He notes that some students drop out of sight without notice because they're often "hanging by a thread."

and I became a high school math teacher for the next 15 years. We moved here just a year ago to help care for family. We've become involved with the Bessemer Library and literacy during this past year. My wife also was an educator, a high school English teacher and then an assistant principal. We both have active minds, we are active people and together we found the Bessemer Library.

My wife started the "Friends of the Library" program and the bookstore that's here. I decided I would get into the literacy business, and I went to M-POWER Ministries, a faith-based service organization, to learn how to tutor. I felt the Bessemer Library could build a program, and I wanted to help make that happen because the need is so great. We began our literacy program in September, and now we have 14 students and eight tutors.

I try to get people to come to the library the next day after they contact me. I want to see them while they have that idea of help fresh in their minds. Then I work with them while I try to find a tutor. When I locate a tutor, I get the student and tutor together. I want them to understand that their relationship is interdependent. That's what will make this program successful—each of them feeling committed to the other.

Many of our adult students are living right on the edge. They often have little control over their lives. I see them do really well, but then something happens, they have to move, and I don't know if that's job-related, or they can't pay their rent, or something happened in the family. All of a sudden they are just gone. Many of them seem to be just hanging on by threads, and if one of those threads breaks, you've lost them.

Most realize that's where they are, and they are trying to do something about it. They believe that improving their reading skills will improve their life.

> **When over one-third of the adult population is unable to read editorial opinions, when millions cannot understand the warning on a pack of cigarettes or comprehend the documents they sign to rent a home, to buy a car, to purchase health insurance, who can persist in the belief that literacy is not political?**
>
> — *Jonathan Kozol,*
>   *Illiterate America*

They believe that reading is the tool for escaping from that little edge they are perched on. My hope for this program is that they will develop enough of a relationship with their tutor so that when something like this happens, they will turn to their tutor and say, "This is what's happening to me." Then maybe the tutor will know some solutions, or maybe call me, and see if there aren't solutions we can come up with, together, to keep them in the program.

The first young man I tutored was about to graduate from high school, and his girl friend found out that he couldn't read. She called the people at M-POWER and asked if they could help him. I told them I could meet with this young man every day for three weeks until school started for his senior year. So I met with him, and I would go over to his house and pick him up and we'd go to McDonald's. I'd buy him breakfast, and we'd work until we felt that we had worn out our welcome, or the lunch crowd came in and it became noisy. Then we would pick up and go over to Wal-Mart, where there's a Subway shop, and we'd buy lunch and sit in a corner and munch on a sandwich and continue our work until mid-afternoon when we were both exhausted. We worked 6-8 hours every day. He was basically at about a first-grade reading level when we started, and we were trying to get him as close to high school level as possible in those three weeks.

Once he started high school, the idea was that he would transition into a literacy program on the south side of the city. He's a very bright young man. He had to be to successfully fake his reading skills for so many years. I think what caused the secret to leak out was that he wanted a driver's license, and he couldn't read enough to take the written test. The two of us never got far enough to successfully read the manual. He was clearly making progress, but he wasn't ready for that.

I learned later that he graduated from high school though he couldn't read. He's still functionally illiterate. That breaks my heart. Here you have the classic example: You have a young person, still with an open and bright mind, unlike some older people where progress comes very slowly. He worked very hard. We covered a lesson an hour, which doesn't happen much with older learners. He improved his word recognition, his comprehension and his understanding of phonics. He had a core capability that he expanded on. I think he was at about the sixth-grade reading level when we finished our three weeks.

The United States is not a literacy super-power.

— *ProLiteracy, 2006*

Functional illiteracy is a serious problem in Alabama. Shortly after I started here the *Birmingham News* reported a story on illiteracy; their banner line for the day was "90,000 illiterate live in the Birmingham area." That's a staggering number, but I believe it. I meet people here, and far too many of them have completed high school, mind you, and they may have a certificate rather than a diploma, but they will say, "Nobody tried to teach me anything. They put me in a corner and kept going, and then passed me on to the next grade." Look at where we are: Our program is barely six months old, and we already have 14 people enrolled in the literacy program. There's another half a dozen who came once or twice to reading sessions, then didn't return.

I think we need to do two things in this state to deal with functional illiteracy. First, we desperately need a new constitution to return some power and decision making to local communities. Second, we need to develop an education program that shouts out to the world: "We are so embarrassed to say, thank God for Mississippi and Louisiana! We are going to stop saying that and start saying: How far are we now from the top? Who cares if we are the number one football team in America! We want to be number one each year in the number of high school graduates who can read!"

Now, don't get me wrong, I'm a football fan, but I recently read the John Grisham novel *Bleachers*. The story takes place in a small town, and a bunch of old football players have returned to the town, for a reunion or something. And they're all sitting around drinking beer and talking about the town, how they don't understand what it is, how they are all just crazy about football and their football team. Football is the most important thing in their lives. And one of them says: It's what happens when you don't have anything else, that's the only thing you can find to be proud of.

When I read that I thought, this needs to be on the front page of every newspaper in Alabama. This is a beautiful state; there's so much to like and love about it. There are so many resources that draw tourists to our state. The medical facility here in Birmingham, it's unbelievable. Yet, so much of our population is just being pushed aside. How our entire state can't be embarrassed by that is beyond me.

My goal with the program here is to fill the space and time at the Bessemer library with readers and tutors, literally around the clock. Look, the library is open 55 hours each week, and we have three available rooms for reading and tutoring. So do the math. We can provide one hour of help each week to 165 people.

We've got 14 in the program now, so we can help 150 more people. We can do a lot more. I want to fill up all those hours and those rooms with people who need reading help and those who can help them.

Stories of Community

Enriching the village

27. The greatest job in the world

The story of **Jackie Wuska Hurt,** chair,
Literacy Council of West Alabama and director of
development, University of Alabama Honors College

MY mom was the mayor of Vestavia Hills, and my
dad worked his entire career at American Cast
Iron Pipe Company. They met as students at the University of Alabama, and I came here for undergraduate
and graduate school. I wasn't really sure what I wanted
to do. I thought about law school, but I ended up
working with the Jefferson County Commission as a
graduate school intern—for two commissioners who
are now under legal investigation. When I was a
student at UA, I was active in student government, and
I really enjoyed it because everyone was working hard
and dedicated. So I thought government work was
what I really want to do with my life. But when I
worked at the local commission level, I realized this
wasn't my interest.

   I returned to the university in a position at Alumni
Hall where I was the director of alumni events and
involved with Homecoming. After that I was director
of the Capstone Engineering Society and did fund-
raising for the Crimson Promenade. I then returned to
my hometown of Birmingham and worked at the
University of Alabama-Birmingham as development
director for the School of Arts and Humanities. In 2003
I became executive director of the Literacy Council,
which is based in Birmingham and serves five counties
in central Alabama. That experience has had a tremendous impact on my career and growth. In 2008, I came

back to UA as development director for the Honors College, and this year I became chair of the Literacy Council of West Alabama.

At the Literacy Council, I was single, I didn't have children and I worked late every night. I usually gave myself Saturday off, but I'd go in Sunday evenings to catch up. I mean, it was such a good cause that you could literally work on it all the time. I remember I'd drop off a grant proposal at 9:28 p.m. at FedEx because they close at 9:30, and then the next morning I was already thinking about what grant proposal I could apply for next. I thrived on the work, and we grew steadily. But the thing that was so great was when someone called your literacy help line and said, "I want to learn to read, I've really got to improve my reading." That brought it home for me: I knew I had the greatest job in the world!

> **In an interview broadcast on *60 Minutes* in June 2007, Iranian President Ahmadinejad highlighted America's "20 percent illiteracy rate" to illustrate our vulnerability.**
>
> — *National Commission on Adult Literacy*

The thing I'm most proud of there, apart from increasing our budget and actually being able to give grants to service providers, is that we started the GED scholarship program. Under this program, the student gave $10 and the Literacy Council provided $40, and this paid admission into the eight-hour GED test. We also reimbursed childcare or other expenses associated with taking the test. To receive the money, the students had to write a short letter explaining why they wanted to take the test, and these made the most compelling stories about why they wanted to learn to read, or to write or speak.

They were so proud of what they accomplished; many of them are in college now, and their stories are the best examples of what can happen to people who believe in themselves and are committed to improving. And I was so touched when the Literacy Council actually named the scholarship for me.

I'm so impressed with what the local council in Tuscaloosa has accomplished in its first few years, and I hope I can share some expertise gained in central Alabama. I'm on the governor's Workforce Investment Board, and the council here is the only one in west Alabama. We need councils like this all over the state. What's being done so well here is coordination of the faith-based efforts and the involvement and leadership of business—that's really crucial.

You know, in Cuba the literacy rate is about 100 percent. You go to school and learn to read, or you cut sugar cane, which is what the prisoners do. I'm not advocating that we become like Cuba, but the problem here is significant, and most don't understand its scope and scale. I mean, how can illiteracy be such a large problem in our society?

I think we have to infuse literacy into every non-profit and charitable organization. Some coalitions, for example, require that each agency funded by United Way must incorporate some literacy initiative into its work. For example, little league baseball teams could include reading components that help kids understand how to read and calculate baseball statistics. Senior citizen agencies could have programs that involve reading aloud to seniors, or provide large print books. This approach requires that every organization makes

Jackie Wuska Hurt combines a career in fund raising for the university with leading regional literacy efforts, and thrives on a heavy workload. Given the sheer size and societal cost of the literacy issue, she advocates building trust first by helping people where they need it most—be it training in nutrition or managing money—and then ensure they also can read and write.

literacy a priority in some sense. We need to infuse literacy into our workplaces, churches, community programs and social activities so that help is available throughout the community.

Literacy is interlinked with so many crucial issues in our society—crime, poverty, homelessness and un-employment, and we pour so much money into trying to deal with these issues, yet they persist. We need to go at what may be the key root to these problems—the ability to read. We need to alert people, we need to scare them, we need to provide a solution and we need to demonstrate to people how they can and must be a part of that solution. It has to be a holistic, systemic approach. I don't know any other way.

A related issue is the shame factor—being embarrassed because you can't read and not wanting people to know you can't read. It's amazing to me that if English is your second language, there is no shame involved—you want to learn to read and speak English. But if English is your first language and you can't read, you are embarrassed and so you don't ask for help. I think that's terribly ironic and sad.

Sometimes it's even difficult to talk about when you personally know an individual. For example, there was a custodian in my church in Birmingham; I'd known him for many years. One day we were doing something in church, and I asked him if he could get a couple of double AA batteries for a camera, or something. And he went away to get them, and it took him a long time. So finally I went to see what he was doing, and I saw him taking out batteries from a box and feeling them, trying to feel what a double AA battery was because he couldn't read. I didn't know he couldn't read, and because I'd known him for so long, I didn't want to say anything directly to him for fear of offending him. I trained someone else to speak with him so that it was more of a professional matter for his career benefit, like "If you improve your reading skills,

> **Of 222 million adults aged 16 or older in the U.S., some 93 million lack literacy at a level needed to enroll in postsecondary education or job training that current and future jobs require.**
>
> — *National Commission on Adult Literacy*

you could do this or that career wise." So it's a very sensitive issue.

Marketing reading programs to people who can't read also is very difficult because we don't normally think of all the threats or fears they may have. So I think you have to build trust first. Maybe you hold a health literacy class or a financial literacy class that's targeted to about a second-grade reading level. People are interested in those things, so that's a starting point for getting people to come forward. You don't emphasize the literacy aspects so much as the benefits of eating or cooking healthy foods, or learning how to balance a budget. Then you can build on that in terms of encouraging people to develop their reading skills as a way to be healthier, or handle money better. It starts with trust.

According to polls and studies in the region, the number one reason people get reading help is to gain a better job, number two is to help your children read and number three is to be able to read the Bible. Literacy just touches our lives in so many ways. One of our tutors in central Alabama worked with a gentleman who wanted to improve his reading so he could get a promotion. Well, his reading and confidence improved in three or four months, so he was promoted. But even more important, this man's son was shipped to Iraq. And with his improved reading skills, he was able for the first time to communicate with his son in Iraq via email. Improved reading touched his life in a way he never imagined.

There was another student who had drug addiction issues and was in a home for women. She was a very intelligent woman, and it became clear that she could really benefit from a GED, so she went to work on that and earned her GED and gained a job. That allowed her to adopt her little sister and take her out of a terrible environment where she was subjected to physical abuse. This lady converted her passion for drugs into passion for education and for moving her sister into a better environment.

Stories like these motivate me, tutors and literacy boards across the state and country to grow and improve and reach out as far as we can. It's the most inspiring work.

28. We are all brothers

The story of **José Cabrera-Vargas**, adult learner, Hoover

I was born in Cueramaro, a small city in Mexico. My father was a musician. He played a small guitar and made music in restaurants and clubs. When I came to America in the 1970s, I lived in Los Angeles. I had three restaurants there—La Sirena Restaurant, La Hacienda and Los Molcahetes—all with Mexican food. I was the owner, the manager, one of the musicians, and a singer, too. I played Veracruz music; if you know La Bamba, you know Veracruz music. It has a Veracruz harp in it, and I played a violin. I did that for many years until the restaurant business went bad in the economy in California.

My wife and I have four children: two boys and two girls. They live in California and Arizona. One girl works in special education. Another works for a large cooling or air conditioning company. Two others work in the Sears Company.

We came to Alabama because there was work here for my mariachi music. I remember the day when I arrived in Alabama; it was March 26, 2000. I remember that date because it was my birthday! When I arrived at the airport, my band members were waiting for me. In the airport bathroom I put on my mariachi suit and big hat, and we went to the restaurant to play the music. I land in the plane and then we go to make the music! We played in several restaurants in Pell City for a long time.

José Cabrera-Vargas opens the door to the literacy center in Hoover, where he and his wife have taken English classes for several years. A musician, José moved to Alabama from California to play in a mariachi band. Communication is key to knowing a new culture, he says, and he laments that he didn't learn English at a younger age.

Many years ago when I went to school in Mexico, one of the teachers asked the class, does anybody want to learn English? And I said no, I didn't need it. If we went to the United States, then we would study English. It would be important then. But now I study English at the school in Hoover.

It is more difficult to learn when you are old. When we come to this country, my oldest daughter was seven years old. In one year and a half, she is speaking English. My second boy was five years old, and he learned to speak English very fast. Now they speak both English and Spanish. So now my wife and I try to learn. We have time now to learn. Before, we worked 17-18 hours a day. My wife was a manager for an apartment complex in Los Angeles, 80-100 apartments. We painted the rooms and cleaned the rooms, everything. We worked hard and had no time to learn English.

Now we go to the Multicultural Resource Center in Hoover for two hours every day to study English. We learn to read, to write and to spell. We know the letters, but the letters in Spanish and English sound different. There are 5 to 10 people in the class, sometimes more. We have been going to classes for about two years.

We also try to help with the school. We clean the carpet. We clean the bathrooms one time each week. We help with anything because we want to help keep the school clean. Some people want the service, but they don't want to help. In life, we have to help. Everybody has to help. I believe that in the world, we are all brothers. We should respect each other and help each other, not make problems.

We want to be part of the American culture, and communication is the key. No? English is the American language. I am happy when you understand the words I say to you. You are happy when I understand the words you say to me. Maybe you don't understand all my words, but I try. Mistakes are okay as long as you try to learn. My wife understands and reads the words better than I do. But speaking is difficult for both of us. We learn the language to become part of this culture.

Reading and speaking English is also important in life. When you go to the bank, or write checks, for example, it is a problem when someone at the bank doesn't speak Spanish. It is more difficult. And when you dial the telephone, they ask if you want English or Spanish. Okay. I push for Spanish. But then we wait and wait and wait for this interpreter, maybe 20 or 30 minutes for someone to speak Spanish. So I want to continue to study English so these are no longer problems. And English is a world language, so when we go to Europe they can understand our words. Many people in Europe speak English.

My speaking and writing and reading are getting better in English. In California, everybody speaks Spanish. But not so many in Alabama and other states speak Spanish. Some people here, they try to speak Spanish to us, but we must still learn to speak and understand English better.

Low literate adults are less likely to vote than strong readers, but become more active in their communities as their reading and writing skills improve.

— *ProLiteracy, 2010a*

I want a future here. I try to get something for my sons, for their future. In 2003 I went to buy six acres of land in Alabama, near Cullman. I went to the real estate office to make the contract in English. But only when we went to sign the final papers, the real estate office had a final interpreter. So I bought the land without fully understanding the contract, until the last minute. Now this land is for my sons: I transferred the property to them. It is beautiful land. My plan is to move to Cullman. There, maybe we rent some of the space for mobile homes. You know, we might have a little business. That is my vision. We need to make some more money to live. So that is my plan for us.

My sons say, come back to California. But I say, why? Why would we want to move back to California? What would I do in California? It's too expensive to live in California. You can't buy a house. You can't find enough work to live.

My wife and I are happy in Alabama. It is a beautiful state. We like it here. We have a small house where we live now, but for my wife and me it's too big. We have some flowers and plants around the house, some little plantitas. We are happy here. In this country, it's a good life for us and our children.

29. It takes a community

The story of **Kristen Bobo,** adult education coordinator for Tuscaloosa County and GED Online, Shelton State Community College

I earned my bachelor's degree at the University of Alabama—a major in human development and family studies and a minor in computer science. After working part time with adult education, I decided that was the place for me. So I went back to school and got my master's in postsecondary education. I'm now 25 years old, a newlywed and the adult education coordinator here at Shelton State. I love my job.

My grandfather dropped out of school in the sixth grade to work on the farm, and he cannot read. So, I saw a lot of characteristics in my students that I saw at home. I know that he always told me, "Don't let anybody that you meet have the problems I do." You see, he has to rely on other people to do his daily activities. For example, like going to a store and writing a check, he would be able to sign it, but he would depend on the people who were checking him out to actually enter the amount on the check. Then my grandmother would have to go back and make sure it was the right amount, that they didn't take advantage of him.

Or, he couldn't write his address. That would frustrate him. If he had a car wreck, for example, how would he tell someone where he lives? He could tell you how to get where he lived, but he couldn't write it down for you. Or, a phone number. He could tell it to you, but he couldn't write it. Things like that.

I became involved with literacy when I was a student at the university. During my senior year, Miss Julia Chancy came and visited my class, and I was required to complete service hours for the class. The Project Literacy program that Miss Chancy talked about was so interesting, and I already worked part time at Shelton, so I thought I could do my volunteer hours at Shelton. When I started tutoring the adults, I just fell in love with the work. I knew that's what I wanted to do.

My first reading student was an older lady who was determined to improve her reading so she could be more active in her Sunday school class and church. So we would have our reading lesson, and at the end of every session we would go over the church bulletin. She would then know what was going on that week, the things she could talk about in class and materials she could take to talk about it. The most exciting moment was when she was able to lead a complete Sunday school lesson. She brought in her book, which was prob-

Adults who dropped out of high school and later enroll in adult education or literacy classes to earn a high school diploma or General Education Degree can increase their earnings by an average of $9,000 a year.

— *ProLiteracy, 2010b*

ably at about a fourth-grade reading level, and she read the entire lesson to the Sunday school class. We had worked at it for weeks, but she did it, and she felt wonderful. It was a personal triumph for her and a very rewarding moment for me.

Kristen Bobo has earned her master's degree but her grandfather couldn't read. Recruited as a volunteer tutor, she loved the experience so much she has now made it her life's work. She urges her students to start with small goals and then build on their achievements. Literacy is a community issue, she says, and requires a community to resolve it.

Another student was a younger woman, exactly the same age as me. We became really good friends. She completed high school with a certificate of attendance, but she couldn't pass the exit exam. She'd completed all 12 years of school, and she wanted to learn to read, even though she had certificate of attendance. She was labeled learning disabled all through school. She wanted to do away with that label, but she needed some help. So she enrolled in GED classes, and her reading level was second grade.

I asked her what her goal was, and she said it was to attend and graduate from the University of Alabama. My eyes got really big. I wanted to help her achieve that goal, but I felt it was unrealistic. However, she's completed the PLUS program, she went into a

GED class, she's signed up to take the GED exam, and now she scores at the 10th-grade reading level. She loves reading and is actually helping others in her family learn to read. To see her go from not wanting to read at all because she was nervous, or thought she would fail, to now reading books two or three times and helping other family members—it's incredible.

Another student I often think about, and he comes by to visit me often, was a 17-year-old boy. He was very rebellious and wanted to be the center of attention. Reading wasn't something he was interested in. We worked for six months before he was arrested and spent a year in jail. He then returned to my reading class because he was ordered to by his probation officer. He had grown up a lot in that year, and he was determined to complete his education so that he could create a better life for himself. Well, he completed his GED in one year and is now in college and pursuing an associate's degree.

Adults confront many barriers to reading, and many who can't read just adapt to *not* being able to read. Retaining adult learners in tutoring programs and education programs is a problem, too, and this is where tutors are so crucial. Adult learners and tutors often build strong relationships. They build trust. So maintaining the same tutor for a student is really important to keeping that student in the program.

Two types of people come to us for help: those who are supported in their learning, or are required to be here, and those who think it sounds like a good idea until they see how much work and time it actually takes. If you have to start with learning the ABCs, it's going to take awhile, and that's discouraging for some. It takes a lot of time outside of the classroom or volunteer session, too. So when they see the time commitment and work that's necessary, many decide they can go on living without being able to read.

When people start, of course they want to know how long it will take them to learn to read. We always start by saying, "Let's see if you can read this far." We give them a placement test. And when they see that test, it scares them, especially if they can't read at all, if they can't answer that first question. So then we say we're going to work together on this, and how much time you study at home, and how much time you want to meet here per week with us, that will all determine how long it might take you. But you can't really provide anyone with a definite length of time required, and that's frustrating to them.

I see students coming in every day who have a dream: They want to enter a certain occupation or have a specific career. Then they sit down to take the test, and they find out or confirm that they can't read, that they need time to improve their reading, and so they become frustrated and their dreams die. That's serious. We try to motivate them to make a new dream, to set a short-term goal, and when that's accomplished, to set another goal, and so forth.

We use different benchmarks to do this. If you fall into the functional illiteracy group, for example, we often create a short-term goal, like a trade. Learn a trade first, and then while you're learning that trade, you're still improving your academic skills. And you have a trade, and then maybe you can go on to your next goal. For many of these people, ability-to-benefit programs are great; they don't require a high school diploma. I mean things like auto body repair, diesel mechanic, barbering. As they make progress, then we set other short-term goals. We never turn away or discourage the bigger, longer-term goal. We just try to create realistic steps to get there.

Most of our students are struggling with other social and economic issues, too. As a tutor, you need to understand these issues and problems and how they influence the lives of the students. Poverty is the number one issue I encounter, and it's closely related to unemployment, especially in today's world. When I first started, employment was not such a big issue. Maybe they didn't have the job they wanted, but they had some work. Right now we're seeing more individuals coming in for help because the job market and economy are so poor. Teen pregnancy is always an issue, too.

Literacy is truly a community issue, and it takes a whole community to resolve it. I believe that in my heart. It's important to always keep in your mind the need to observe others, and, if you see someone having difficulty reading, maybe just talk to that person, open a door. We can all reach out to others.

My mom taught me that, with anyone I meet in life, I should provide a sense of support to that person because they may not have it at home. They may not even have a home. But we all need support; we all need a network. So with each student I meet, I try to give them my undivided attention, to show them they count and they are important to us.

We can provide support in this community. We can deal with this as a community.

30. Literacy and economy

The story of **Johnnie Aycock,** president, Chamber of Commerce of West Alabama

IF I sound passionate about literacy, it's because I am. Literacy is at the core of economic vitality and capability in this country, and I want to make that economic case today. But first I want to tell you how I arrived at that belief, which grows out of my background and experiences in the business and political worlds.

My dad was a retailer who owned a radio and TV appliance store in Decatur, Alabama, for more than 60 years. It was called Aycock's Radio Shack before there was a Radio Shack chain. The chain came to Decatur one time and threatened to sue my dad over the name of his store, but my dad sued back and won. He didn't want money, just an apology, which he received.

I went to Auburn University and majored in economics and minored in English and music. I was well rounded only because I switched majors so many times. Then I returned to Decatur and went into banking for about five years. I also worked voluntarily with the local Chamber of Commerce and became interested in economic development. I moved to Gadsden as assistant manager of the Chamber and director of the downtown development corporation. A year later I was named executive VP of the Chamber in Gadsden. I was there about seven years; we built a good organization and did more industrial development work.

During this time I became very active with the Jaycees, and I eventually became state president of the organization and then national VP of the Jaycees in

Miami. This got me very interested in political work, and I went to work in Washington, D.C., with the National Association of Manufacturers. I was the southern political director for two years, and that experience proved invaluable over the years.

After that, I went to work for the Jackson, Mississippi, Chamber of Commerce as their lobbyist. I worked closely with the governor, who was a champion for educational reform in the state, and that's where I really began to understand the close connection between education and economic development. In 1983 I became president of the Chamber in Tuscaloosa, and I'm still here today.

> **The U.S. ranks 51st in literacy among all United Nations members.**
>
> — *Bob Cleckler, Let's End Our Literacy Crisis*

I brought with me my experiences with, and concerns for, education reform and we started the Adopt-a-School program, which has been a major component of what we've done since then—K-12 education and higher education. In a sense, the Literacy Council of West Alabama started by accident. I think I'm like many people; I just imagined that everyone can read. In 2007, Sandra Ray, who was on the state school board and then president of the Rotary Club, wanted to do a literacy project. So I explored other Rotary Clubs and found that most were buying books for libraries, conducting reading programs for kids and other kinds of one-time projects.

Then I started looking around to see which organizations in the area were engaged in literacy, and no one seemed to know. Finally, I called Fran Turner at Shelton State Community College, and she told me that Project Literacy was headquartered at Shelton. So we discussed some projects and realized that Project Literacy was largely unknown and there were actually dozens of organizations that had some connection to literacy in the area. Even the National Guard had a program. The problem was that nobody knew about these service providers, they were difficult to contact, they didn't know about each other and they seemed disconnected from the community. They had no money and no visibility.

So I concluded that we had a bigger problem than the Rotary project, or just buying some books. To learn more, I called Steve Hannum at the Literacy Council in Birmingham, and I spent a half day with Steve and Jackie Hurt, who was then the director of the Literacy Council, the only one in the state of Alabama. To this day the state does not have a statewide literacy initiative, and I think we are the only state in the country that does not. This is tragic to me.

Steve and Jackie were unbelievably helpful, and we began to give thought to developing a sustainable literacy program in west Alabama. In early 2008 we held a literacy summit in Tuscaloosa and began to try to connect the pieces. The summit was phenomenally successful; more than 400 folks from all over Alabama attended. I think we hit a nerve with this issue, which is a phantom issue to me because it's always been there, but it's virtually invisible. It's also hard to define, it's difficult to locate and reach adults who need help, and literacy applies not just to reading and understanding, but also to writing, math and more and more to technology skills.

Johnnie Aycock, the representative voice of business in west Alabama, has become a champion of literacy on a strategic level, trying to make this "phantom issue" highly visible. He understands that to attract new jobs a community needs an educated workforce. And he fears that, as a nation, we're actually regressing on this front.

Then we made the connection among literacy skills, workforce preparation and workforce capacity and economic development. These are tightly interwoven, and they affect the growth and competitiveness of businesses. You cannot disconnect these factors; you cannot put literacy in a box off to the side. It is integrated and interwoven.

So out of the literacy summit the idea grew that to sustain this initiative, we needed a west Alabama literacy council, which we created that summer. We began with a wonderful set of board members in 2008, we developed a service provider network, we held some workshops, we started an annual recognition luncheon, we've begun to create awareness and now we've received a $250,000 federal appropriation through Congressman Artur Davis. So we have some legs—and a lot more work to do.

Literacy is deeply connected to our economic system, but no one is really making an economic case for literacy. Too many people simply don't understand the economic basis of literacy. Here's one staggering fact: One out of four people in Alabama is functionally illiterate. They can't read and understand their work manual. They can't read instructions, read a prescription for their child or read a child's book to their kids. They can't read signs, a menu, a newspaper or even the Bible.

> **The minimum cost of illiteracy of $590 billion per year along with additional crime costs linked to illiteracy totals at least $5,186 per taxpayer each year.**
>
> *— Bob Cleckler, Let's End Our Literacy Crisis*

What does that mean in the workplace? Well, how does an employer help an individual grow on the job and be more effective and productive if they can't read? If an employee can't function to a level to help that employer grow and be successful, then the employee loses, the company loses and the community loses.

Here are some other facts: The number one cause of high school dropouts is lack of reading ability. Also, if you can't read at the fourth-grade level by the fourth grade, you are lost because at the fourth-grade level students transition from learning to read to reading to learn. In addition, literacy is a major thread in many social and economic problems like crime, poverty and homelessness. And we know that reading literacy is connected to math literacy, technology literacy, writing literacy and so forth.

So it continues to baffle me that literacy is such a phantom issue and that our businesses across the state don't pay more attention to it. It's a statewide problem that puts pressure on the public sector and reduces workforce capacity. So if we want economic growth, we need workforce capacity. We need people who can read, learn, understand, grow and contribute. What can't we understand about that?

I'll give you two examples close at hand. First, I'm told by a reliable source that one quarter of the workforce in the city of Tuscaloosa—people who work for the Tuscaloosa city government—would be considered functionally illiterate. Second, 75 percent of small business owners in Alabama tell us that many job applicants are functionally illiterate and can't be hired. How do they know? Because they can't even fill out a job application. How tragic is that? This makes it extremely difficult to attract new businesses or grow existing businesses, which actually account for about 80 percent of job growth.

But employers don't seem to understand: They are not addressing the issue, most communities are not addressing the issue and the state is not addressing the issue. It just baffles me. And the really bad news is that functional illiteracy is not declining; it's actually growing in this country. As our existing workforce retires, it is being replaced by a workforce that is less educated, less literate—for the first time in the history of this country. How can that be? Why have we let that happen? How can we compete and grow and be successful in an uncertain future if millions of our workers are functionally illiterate?

I believe Tuscaloosa needs to do four things to address this crucial issue. First, we must continue to raise awareness and stimulate greater involvement by a number of people, but especially employers. Second, we need to integrate literacy everywhere, whether in the United Way, Junior League, Rotary Club, YMCA, all of these and others. Each individual organization needs a literacy strategy. Third, this community could lead in moving the issue onto the state's agenda. Maybe with the Literacy Council in Birmingham we could influence strategies in the new administration to make literacy improvement a significant theme. We also could hold another summit next year and take the literacy message statewide. Fourth, we need to stabilize the Literacy Council of West Alabama and ensure we are funded sufficiently so that we can continue to operate and become more effective. We need to make our council sustainable, which means funding, and we need a strategic plan, good board members, measurement and so forth.

These are some important steps for our community. But what could we be? That's always the most important question, isn't it? Not what we are, but what we could be or become. I think we can be a lot more. I hope we will become a lot more. But it has to start with people who care and with political willpower. We need more political willpower to get us there.

Other faces

THE faces of people needing help, and those willing to offer it, are as varied in West Alabama as in any community. These photographs capture a few of the hundreds of other people on the front lines of the literacy movement.

Experienced tutor "Miss Tommie" Blanton spends hours with her regular students at the Birmingham Literacy Council office—in a classroom sponsored by a business that depends on a clientele of readers.

Martha Brown reviews a lesson with Gary Freeman (top), at the Bessemer Public Library, which features a new wing with classrooms serving the active literacy program. Later, in the same classroom, Maso Garrett jokes with Dontay Houston. Maso notes that many tutors end up serving as life coaches for their students, helping them deal with everyday issues that might otherwise impede their success.

Linda Holt helped launch and continues to serve as a volunteer at the Friends Bookstore at the Bessemer Library. While patrons can check out books for free from the library, they can purchase paperbacks for only 50 cents and other books for $1 at the bookstore.

Maria Cabrera has regularly attended English language classes at Hoover's Multicultural Resource Center with her husband, José, for years. The two show their appreciation by helping to maintain the center.

Epilogue:
The challenge to make a difference

I started this last chapter in the spring of 2011, some months after completing most of the interviews that produced these stories. I wish I could say that all of the stories have happy endings—that all of the adult learners are making progress and all of the tutors are still tutoring. But change and uncertainty are stark realities on the front lines of literacy because the process of coming to read for most adults is elongated, dynamic and fraught with pitfalls.

Some adult learners like Cheryl, José, David, Yolanda, Kayla Ann and Steven continue to bring their dreams of reading to life, day by day, even as they reflect often on the daunting work that remains. For the time being they accept that progress is far slower than they would like. However, they make enough progress, or they come to simply enjoy the process of learning to read and their interactions with tutors and other students, so that they continue.

For others like Odella, Latonya, Charnessa and Kimberly, however, the day arrives when they fail to show up for their tutoring sessions. They can't be reached. They are gone. Maybe their work schedules changed, they relocated to another city, or they were forced to deal with more pressing economic or family needs. Perhaps they fall back into past practices or habits, or simply grow too discouraged by the height of the mountain they are climbing. Maybe their dreams of reading are pushed aside temporarily, or extinguished. They might return. They might not.

Tutors also change. Tommie, Neil, Joyce, Dave and Richard are still tutoring, and they may continue to do so for years. Others have moved on. Robert landed a new job, bought a car, moved into an apartment and withdrew from tutoring following completion of his six-month commitment. He's working hard to live the "square John" life for which he prayed. Grant departed Birmingham for Auburn University, where he's pursuing his dream of earning a technical writing degree so he can "do even more things in the world." Lauren travelled to France for a semester to continue her international studies; Mary Lena relocated to Tennessee; and Louise completed her graduate degree and landed a job with a communication agency in Birmingham. She has continued her volunteer work with literacy there by joining a local community service provider.

The connectors are still hard at it, though Johnnie retired from the Chamber of Commerce at the end of 2010. He has taken up another challenge that includes an ongoing commitment to fighting illiteracy at the state level. The Literacy Council of West Alabama in Tuscaloosa appointed its first executive director in the fall of 2010, received office space at Shelton State Community College, and is moving ahead with a nine-county strategic planning effort. The devastating tornado that struck Tuscaloosa on April 27, 2011, claimed 50 lives and destroyed more than 5,000 homes and businesses. Part of the rebuilding effort includes construction of several family literacy houses in the most heavily damaged neighborhoods.

The Literacy Council in Birmingham wrestled with serious budget cuts in 2010 and developed new ways to help meet the great needs in central Alabama. Dave Holt's adult tutoring program at the Public Library in Bessemer continues to evolve, while the Catholic Social Services Multicultural Resource Center in Hoover steadfastly pursues its mission. That center and other ESL programs in Alabama, however, have been significantly impacted by the state's tough new immigration law, currently under legal challenge.

New faces also appeared on the literacy front lines in central Alabama, as Nick Miles demonstrated in his photography. Lillian, Joannie and Aminata are new students in reading programs in Birmingham. In Bessemer, Dave Holt recruited Martha Brown, Joyce Binion and Maso Garrett as new tutors to help with new adult learners Gary, Lucretia, Dontay and Kayla Ann, among others. They are all coming to know each other and to find their way forward.

The UA student group that Louise Crow led, Literacy is the Edge (LITE), recruited 245 university students who went on to become ESL teaching assistants or reading tutors for adults and children in Tuscaloosa. The group carried out new recruiting campaigns in fall 2010 and 2011, yielding more than 1,300 student and community volunteers to help fight illiteracy. LITE also created communication materials to support Dave Holt and the adult literacy program at the Bessemer Public Library, as well as the 2012 marketing campaign in west Alabama.

It should come as no surprise that change marks the literacy struggle on the front lines because change is a constant in many things in life. Most of us hold strong feelings about change—we like it, we don't like it, it makes us angry or sad or happy. More important than our feelings about change, however, is the relationship we adopt with it: What do we do with change? What do we do with the opportunity and challenge we have as individuals to make change happen that might enrich the lives of others?

As William Drayton said, "Change starts when someone sees the next step." This is an enormously positive perception of change because each of us can be the "someone" who "sees the next step." Each of us can be an agent for change in our communities and workplaces. We can take that next step, and then we can encourage others to take that step. We will never gain ground on the front lines of literacy if we are unwilling to take on the challenge of change and to model that change for others.

This book has tried to engage you by personalizing illiteracy and presenting the voices and faces of people in west and central Alabama who are engaged on the front lines every day. Some have taken the step to gain redemption or to act on a personal commitment or obligation to another. Others have been moved by the opportunities that literacy presents, or by desires to enrich communities and neighborhoods. But all 30 individuals share the knowledge and the truth of functional illiteracy: It is real. It has a face, it has a voice and it has a name. It lives in your neighborhood and touches many lives, including your life. You can find it in church, in the grocery store and in the Dollar General. It exacts real individual, social, political and economic costs in your community. And it's spreading.

Functional illiteracy is increasing, and our corresponding collective national literacy is declining. For the first time in U.S. history the new generation of younger adults is less educated than the previous generation. The National Commission on Adult Literacy (2008) claims this is due to three factors:

1. The rapid growth of immigration from non-English speaking countries,
2. An adult education system that is out of date and out of touch with current and future needs, and
3. A K-12 education system that is failing the nation. As a result, the commission contends that more than 90 million American adults aged 16 or older lack literacy skills at a level needed to enroll in postsecondary education, or in job training that current jobs require and that will be even more crucial in future jobs.

But too much of a focus on economic concerns, and they are substantial, masks other literacy issues and values that are deeply meaningful to individuals, as Deborah Brandt has argued compellingly (2001, 2009). She contends that "the standards for literacy are always rising and our supply of literacy is in perpetual short-fall" (2009, p. xi). Global economic competition and rapid change and corresponding new requirements for literacy teaching and learning have "destabilized" the overall value of literacy so that the shortfall becomes a constant:

> The growing entanglement of literacy with economic productivity not only affects how reading and writing are learned and practiced. It also shapes the rationales for acquiring literacy, how it is understood, valued and evaluated (2009, p. xii).

In her earlier work, Brandt (2001) examined how people came to learn to read and write in their lives. She discovered a rich network of people and channels that were involved outside of the formal education system, e.g., parents and grandparents, neighbors, teachers, librarians, clubs and unions, as well as television, newspapers and appointment calendars (2009, p. xiii). The economic imperative that appears to drive many discussions of literacy today competes with these networks and may diminish other profoundly important non-economic values for individuals which are linked to reading:

> If anything, people's testimonies attest to the deep personal valuing of literacy for dignity, connection, continuity, development, faith, pleasure, action, and legacy. (Brandt, 2009, p. xiv).

Thus, literacy is much more than economic currency. Literacy nourishes dignity, hope, community involvement and citizenship.

So if we cannot wait for the government to act, and if we cannot teach every young child to read at an acceptable level in our schools, what can we do? Can we see the next step? Can we take it? I believe our best hope is to attack the problem at the neighborhood level, as more and more communities are beginning to do. We can embrace and deal with functional illiteracy at the grassroots level and ground it in the existing infrastructures which serve individuals in our communities—churches, day care centers, libraries and other social and civic groups—and which are known and trusted to those who need help. This represents a way to sustain and support the "personal valuing of literacy" in the senses that Brandt describes. Though this approach may be slow, it represents the best chance to eradicate illiteracy because it takes place within familiar structures in our communities and because we can personally invest in it.

At this level, we must first increase community awareness of functional illiteracy. In the past two years I've talked to hundreds of people in the country about functional illiteracy, and only a handful of them are even aware of the seriousness of this issue. Most are surprised and disbelieving. Students, church and civic groups, libraries and literacy councils, among others, can lead communication efforts by bringing the problem to life for others in the community through local media channels and special events and activities for targeted publics.

We also need to identify and recruit those who need and want help and provide the encouragement and the support systems that create the best conditions for their success. How's this best done? Well, not through print advertisements and booklets. There is a role for television and radio, but perhaps the best approaches are through those existing organizations that serve them, that is, the churches, day-care centers, grocery stores and other in-community locations where they gather and are able to receive personal communications. Face-to-face communication among those who trust each other is the strongest mobilizer.

Kozol (1985) provides a rich example of this in his discussion of "foot-walkers," or "people who can read people," as described by a woman in Cleveland in this passage:

> How do you reach them? You cannot do it by sitting downtown and mailing out brochures. You need to find the kind of person who can walk the neighborhood—someone with a heart and soul. A foot-walker. Someone like that would know very quickly who was illiterate and who was not. That person has got to be able to overcome the illiterate's terror of

the outside world, as well as the feeling that there's nothing out there they could even want. Sojourner Truth said, "I cannot read, but I can read people." So, too, can many of the poorest people in their own communities. We had better send out people who are not afraid that somebody might have the wit to read a message in their eyes. This is a tremendous challenge: to be unafraid to speak to the poor of reading problems in their midst because we are not frightened to be read ourselves and to be discovered lacking in conviction (p. 103-104).

This passage reminds us that literacy is a shared community endeavor, and perhaps the richest gains on the front lines of literacy are made in programs that involve parents, children, neighborhoods, services and sustainable community initiatives. Such programs affect motivation, skills development, attitudes and even social skills and connections or social networks. The Literacy Powerline advocates this approach in its motto: "100 percent literacy through 100 percent community engagement."

Finally, you are needed on the front lines. Millions of American adults need to step up to the front lines and personally engage this issue. How? Here are eight things you can do to make a positive difference:

1. **Become informed.** Learn about the prevalence of illiteracy in your community. What service providers are available? What adult education programs or GED opportunities exist? Is there a reading or tutoring program? The local library is a great starting point for information and for becoming involved. In addition, many organizational websites provide comprehensive information and resources, including ProLiteracy, Literacy Power-

line, the National Commission on Adult Literacy, the National Institute for Literacy and the U.S. Department of Education, among others.

2. **Inform others and spread the word.** Knowledge empowers individuals and groups to act. Help make others aware of the issue locally and what it means in your community. Become an advocate for literacy awareness. Speak with your neighbors and then talk it up in your church, clubs and groups. Write letters to the editor of the local newspaper. Join Facebook or other online social networks that include literacy groups and discussion forums. Help feed the much needed national conversation.

3. **Learn to recognize the signs** of functional illiteracy and lend a hand when someone needs help writing out a check, understanding food or prescription drug labels, or understanding menu items at restaurants. Your help may be a first step in building a friendship or encouraging someone to seek help. As Julia Chancy said, that first step toward coming to read is a giant leap for those who can't read.

4. **Make a financial contribution** to literacy at the local level. Service providers and libraries have undergone savage budget cuts in the current economic climate, and adult literacy receives meager government funding compared to other social programs. If budget allocations signal a government's priorities, then adult education is not a priority at the federal, state or local levels despite its documented links to crime, poverty, unemployment and other serious social issues. We cannot

wait on governments at any level since they are increasingly bankrupt and beleaguered.

5. **Donate books, magazines,** videos, tapes, computers and other literacy materials to service providers, schools, libraries, churches and day-care centers. Millions of American homes are bereft of books, magazines and newspapers. There is literally nothing to read. Give the gift of words.

6. **Encourage your church, company,** civic group or club to support or adopt a library, service provider, a school class or an entire community school. Volunteer your time to help with events, raise funds, collect books or read to children.

7. **Become a tutor** for an adult or child in your community, or volunteer to assist with ESL programs. This is the most wonderful gift. It only requires a few hours each week, and there's no finer thing than making a positive difference in the life of another. Retiree Dave Holt developed the adult tutoring program at the public library in Bessemer and personally recruited 15 adult tutors and more than 20 adult learners in six months. Why did he do it? "Because the need was great, and I had time on my hands," he said. "I wanted to help others discover the joys and benefits of reading that I discovered in school in International Falls, Minnesota, so many years ago."

8. **If you're a high school or college teacher, speak to this issue in your classes.** Add a service-learning component to class and get students involved in tutoring, making posters, raising funds, reading to young children and so forth. Plan and carry out a campaign to tell others in the commu-

nity about illiteracy. Students at the University of Alabama formed an advocacy group in 2008 that has since recruited more than 2,000 students and community members to become reading and math tutors for adults and children, assist with ESL programs and support library and reading activities in the community. Dealing with real problems is a powerful form of learning that builds self-confidence, listening skills, teamwork and a sense of accomplishment. It also may stimulate a volunteer mentality in students that will carry over into active community involvement in later years.

Every action and every step counts, no matter how large or small. On a large scale, Michelle and David Baldacci, the bestselling author, have funded literacy projects in more than 30 states through their Wish You Well Foundation in Virginia (wishyouwellfoundation.org). On a very personal level, Sherry Beth "Aunt B" Dobbins of Moulton, Alabama, encourages children to read by dressing as characters from children's books when she drives her truck on her ice cream route (Windham, 2010). Her ice cream shop is filled with toys and reading and coloring books for children, which they can read in the shop or take home if they wish. She does this to get kids excited about reading and education.

When I began my journey with this book, I imagined that I would interview 15-20 adult learners and their collective and compelling stories would become my story of literacy in west and central Alabama. But I soon realized that this approach would produce an incomplete story because the adult learners talked so much and so fondly of their tutors and their importance not only in their reading work, but in their daily lives. I came to understand that an adult learner is one partner in a crucial three-way relationship with tutors and connectors. So the real story of literacy is about each individual and his or her relationships with others in the triangle, what each partner brings to the table and the communities of identities that may form. We discovered how Miss Tommie and her adult students created a community of learning in Birmingham through their stories and their growing relationships. We learned how Julia Chancy intersected the lives of many tutors and adult learners in Tuscaloosa, and how Dave Holt brought literacy to life for adult learners and tutors in Bessemer.

Learners make meaning and acquire understanding through the close relationships they form with tutors, who also make meaning and acquire understanding through their close relationships with their students. They become friends. They build trust. They come to share some parts of their lives, hopes and dreams. Connectors enrich the relationship by matching tutors and learners and providing a supportive framework for their interactions, or creating exciting and fun environments for reading like Aunt B Dobbins.

The relationships formed by these three partners in literacy represent the rich and vital core of opportunity for success in reading. Creating this core does not require vast new financial resources, grand strategies or new buildings. It just requires human capital in the form of three partners, and you can become one of them. You are needed to build this opportunity for success. You are needed to make a relationship and make a difference.

I came to believe years ago that the most important moments in our lives inevitably occur in special interactions with others. Nothing has convinced me otherwise. The most meaningful and memorable moments are created when we enter the life of another and make a positive difference in that person's life, or when another person makes a positive difference in our life. The experience is profound and unforgettable. At these times, we are able to strip out everything else, all of the frantic daily concerns that normally overwhelm our thoughts, so that we then reach that core of opportunity to make a meaningful difference. We are able to step outside of that small box of ourselves and open up to the rich possibility of the other and what together we might accomplish in a truly transformational space that we have created.

Nothing brings greater satisfaction in life. Nothing brings greater insight into life and who we can be and what we might achieve if we but choose to engage with others. I hope you will engage and make a difference on the front lines of literacy in Alabama, or wherever you live. As Odella so aptly put it, "You can do it. I can do it. We can do it."

— Bruce K. Berger
  January 2012

References

Alabama Poverty Project. (2009, October 6). *Poverty in Alabama: The Facts*. Birmingham, AL: Alabama Poverty Project.

Alabama State Workforce Development Council. (1997). *Workforce Illiteracy in Alabama: Report of the Survey* [Abstract of Eric #404559]. Retrieved from http://www.eric.ed.gov

Baldacci, D. (2010, July 11). Changing lives through books. *Parade Magazine*, p. 17.

Brandt, D. (2009). *Literacy and learning: Reflections on writing, reading and society*. San Francisco: Jossey-Bass.

Brandt, D. (2001). *Literacy in American Lives*. New York: Cambridge University Press.

Brotzen, F. (2008, May 22). Writer Carlos Fuentes calls for Roosevelt-inspired approach to solve global woes at Baker Institute lecture. Retrieved from http://stage.media.rice.edu/media/NewsBot.asp?MODE=VIEW&ID=11043&SnID=18485

Calefati, J. (2009, January 13). Little progress on adult education. *U.S. News & World Report*. Retrieved from http://www.usnews.com

Cleckler, B. C. (2008). *Let's End Our Literacy Crisis* (Revised Ed.]. Salt Lake City, UT: American University & Colleges Press.

Early-To-Learn.com. (2010). The Staggering Costs of Illiteracy. Retrieved from http://www.early-to-learn.com/illiteracy.html

Education-Portal.com. (2007, September 20). Grim Illiteracy Statistics Indicate Americans Have a Reading Problem. Retrieved from http://education-portal.com/articles/

Education-Portal.com. (2007, July 24). Illiteracy: The Downfall of American Society. Retrieved from http://education-portal.com/articles/

Fisher, W. R. (1978). Toward a logic of good reasons. *Quarterly Journal of Speech, 64,* 376-384.

Fisher, W. R. (1987). *Human communication as narration: Toward a philosophy of reason, virtue, and action.* Columbia: University of South Carolina Press.

Haigler, K., and others. (1994, October). *Literacy Behind Prison Walls: Profiles of the Prison Population from the National Adult Literacy Survey.* Retrieved from http://www.eric.ed.gov/PDFS/ED377325/pdf.

Haley, A. (1990, September 2). *Parade Magazine,* p. 28.

Hovey, S. (1982). *Functional Illiteracy* [Abstract of Eric #224030]. Retrieved from http://www.eric.ed.gov

Kozol, J. (1986). *Illiterate America.* New York: Plume.

Leech, M., and Hansen, J. (2009), November 22). Alabama students struggle to read. *The Birmingham News,* pp. A1, A10.

Literacy Powerline. (2010). Retrieved from http://www.literacypowerline.com/resources/facts-stats

Literacy Powerline. (2009). Literacy-2009 National Community Literacy Leadership Conference, Buffalo [PowerPoint slides]. Retrieved from http://www.literacypowerline.com/resources/online-resources

M-POWER Ministries. (2010). Retrieved from http://www.mpowerministries.org/literacy.html

MSN Encarta. (2010). Functional literacy definition. Retrieved from http://encarta.msn.com/dictionary_1861690879/functional_literacy.html

National Center for Education Statistics. (2010). Fast Facts. Retrieved from http://nces.ed.gov/fastfacts/display.asp?id=69

National Commission on Adult Literacy. (2008, June 26). *Reach Higher America: Overcoming Crisis in the U.S. Workforce.* Retrieved from http://www.nationalcommissiononadultliteracy.org/report.html

ProLiteracy. (2010a). The Impact of Literacy. Retrieved from http://www.ProLiteracy.org/NetCommunity/Page.aspx?pid=370&srcid=345

ProLiteracy. (2010b). Statement of Adult Learner Rights. Retrieved from http://www.ProLiteracy.org/NetCommunity/Page.aspx?pid=555&srcid=345

ProLiteracy. (2006). The State of Adult Literacy 2006. Retrieved from http://www.ProLiteracy.org/NetCommunity/Document.Dot?id=14

State of the Village Report. (2005). Retrieved from http://www.odt.org/popvillage.htm

The Talking Page Literacy Organization. (2007). The National Illiteracy Action Project 2007-2012. Retrieved from http://www.talkingpage.org/NAP2007.pdf

The Education Trust. (2005, June). *Getting Honest About Grad Rates: How States Play the Numbers and Students Lose* [Report]. Washington, DC: The Education Trust.

Tippo, G. (2010, March 24). Students' reading scores show little progress. Retrieved from http://www.usatoday.com

Tuscaloosa Chamber of Commerce. (2010). Retrieved from http://tuscaloosachamber.com/literacy/facts.html

U.S. Department of Education. (1998). *The State of Literacy in America* [Report]. Washington, DC: U.S. Department of Education.

U.S. Department of Education. (1993, December). *Adult Literacy in America*. Retrieved from http://www.nald.ca/fulltext/report2/rep15-01.htm

Washington County Literacy Council. (2010). The Impact of Illiteracy. Retrieved from http://washingtoncountyliteracycouncil.org/

Windham, A. (2010, August 1). Ice cream used to promote reading. *The Tuscaloosa News*, pp. B1, B5.

Wish You Well Foundation. (2010). Retrieved from http://wishyouwellfoundation.org/

Bruce K. Berger, Ph.D., is professor of advertising and public relations at the University of Alabama. He is a member of the board of directors of the Plank Center for Leadership in Public Relations and a trustee of the Institute for Public Relations. For the past four years he has served as a member of the board of directors of the Literacy Council of West Alabama, and faculty advisor to Literacy is the Edge (LITE), the student advocacy group at the University of Alabama. Previously, he worked in corporate communications for 20 years. He and his wife, Joan, live in west Alabama.

Nickerson B. Miles is a vice president of enterprise communications for TIAA-CREF, a financial services firm serving the not-for-profit community. An avid photographer for more than 40 years, he has traveled and shot in five of the world's seven continents. He and his wife, Maggie, live in northern New Jersey.

WordWorthyPress, LLC
11553 Council Barber Blvd.
Northport, AL 35475

Note: All profits from the sale of this book are donated to the Literacy Council of West Alabama and the Literacy Council in Birmingham.

CPSIA information can be obtained at www.ICGtesting.com
Printed in the USA
LVOW131152121012

302567LV00007B/3/P